W9-CKA-298

User's Guide to the Media

For Charles Oxley
Now he dwells where all his wars are won.

Frameworks for Living

User's Guide to the Media

David Porter

Inter-Varsity Press

Inter-Varsity Press
38 De Montfort Street,
Leicester LE1 7GP,
England

Distributed in Australia by
ANZEA Publishers.
Australian ISBN 0-85892-399-8

British Library Cataloguing in Publication Data

Porter, David, *1945-*
User's guide to the media.
1. Mass media. Christian viewpoints
I. Title   II. Series
261.5′6

ISBN 0-85110-790-7

Set in Baskerville
Typeset in Great Britain by Compuset, Belfast
Design and illustration by Spring Graphics,
Saintfield, N. Ireland
Printed in Great Britain by Collins, Glasgow.

Inter-Varsity Press is the book publishing division of the
Universities and Colleges Christian Fellowship (formerly the
Inter-Varsity Fellowship), a student movement linking
Christian Unions in universities and colleges throughout the
United Kingdom and the Republic of Ireland, and a member
movement of the International Fellowship of Evangelical
Students. For information about local and national activities
write to UCCF, 38 De Montfort Street, Leicester LE1 7GP.

Contents

1. The media, a way of life 8

2. TV soap opera —
  windowing the world 20

3. Unmasking adverts 36

4. The news media — telling the truth . . . 50

5. The media as preachers 64

6. Living with the media 78

> . . . there is no
> time or place in
> which we can
> temporarily
> relinquish our
> Christian faith.

Preface

This is a book for today's Christians. It talks about today's world.

The media have a lot to do with leisure and recreation, but for Christians, it's an urgent subject. If we are going to be effective for Jesus Christ in today's world we have to get to grips with the media. If we are going to follow Jesus, it isn't a soft option.

In this book we'll be talking about the media; understanding them, listening and looking with care, being aware, and controlling the place they have in our lives instead of allowing them to control us. It's a practical book, and there are a number of practical projects and exercises suggested in it.

Two things before we start, however. It's essential for Christians to understand the media — but it's not all hard work. It doesn't mean that you'll never be able to listen to *Newsbeat* or watch *EastEnders* because you'll be too busy taking notes. What we're talking about is a way of looking at things, a biblical perspective, not a GCSE paper in an obscure subject.

And secondly, this book isn't an invitation to burn your *TV Times* and start taking the *Financial Times* every morning. I wrote it because I like and enjoy the media. I hope that it will increase your enjoyment of them too.

I'd like to acknowledge the help and advice of too many people to list individually here. However, I want to mention Tim Dean, with whom I've talked media for many years, and Prabhu Guptara, who has provided information, literature, and advice.

And thanks to my wife Tricia, who has put up with a media invasion in our rather tiny home while the book was being written.

David Porter

chapter one

The media, a way of life

Deirdre Barlow dragged her suitcases down the stairs and flung them on to the hall floor. She pushed open the door of the living-room. Her husband was staring into space with a grim, fixed expression. He did not look up when she came in.

'Right. I'm off.' Her voice was flat and tired.

'All right.' He raised his eyes bleakly. 'Just don't you think, when you walk out of that front door, that you're *ever* coming back.'

'I won't,' Deirdre retorted, and stormed out. He buried his face in his hands and sobbed harshly.

The door re-opened. Deirdre's face was streaked with tears. 'Ken — I couldn't go

through that front door . . . please, don't make me go . . .'

Ken rose to his feet and reached for her. They clasped each other wordlessly. The camera glided into a close-up as they wept in each other's arms.

In half-deserted pubs throughout Britain, spellbound viewers broke into loud cheers. In homes up and down the land, the tension eased.

In a major football stadium, the crowd turned from the action on the pitch to applaud the news that was flashed onto the electronic scoreboard. Ken and Deirdre were back together.

All over the country a third of the population was watching. And tabloid journalists all over Fleet Street sighed for the end of a good story, which had filled hundreds of column-inches for many weeks. Once again *Coronation Street* had exerted its massive appeal.

It's a media-mad world

The media hold the minds and hearts of millions. The episode just quoted is from television soap opera, but there are hundreds of similar examples in all the media.

Gossip columnists in the popular Press entertain vast readerships by retailing trivial details of the rich and glamorous.

What possible importance to us is the fact that the second son of Lord and Lady So-and-So went to Mustique with the star of a certain West End stage success? If it were not told us in the media, we wouldn't know, and our lives would not be poorer in any way.

But it is in the media, and so it is of absorbing fascination for us.

It was the media that made so many of us into computer enthusiasts. The British are among the world leaders in home computer ownership. Not so long ago, a computer was a mysterious device in a steel cabinet, attended by white-coated experts. Now most domestic owners use them to play games on. Sir Clive Sinclair started the revolution, but newspapers, advertising and television made it succeed.

The media make selected people into 'personalities'. A weatherman with an amusing accent, a rotund astrologist, a beautiful news-reader, a scientist with a German accent — all achieve cult status.

Making time for the media

Which of the following have you done today?

Watched TV ☐ (*time spent*   )
Listened to the radio ☐ (*time spent*   )
Browsed through adverts ☐ (*time spent*   )
Read a newspaper ☐ (*time spent*   )
Read a magazine ☐ (*time spent*   )
Used any other media ☐ (*time spent*   )

The average weekly media consumption in Britain is approximately 75 hours per person. What do you estimate yours to be?

But their success extends far beyond their original expertise. As media celebrities, their opinions are sought and respected on any subject under the sun. How do they attain that position?

The media make them successful, simply by making them part of the daily lives of millions of people just like you and me.

How can twenty million people be wrong?

Everybody's talking about the media today. Books are written, research is carried out, college courses are provided, and the media themselves (who are fond of self-scrutiny) often join in the discussion.

Many people are suggesting that there are problems with the media. It's claimed that they influence people in harmful ways, that they are antisocial, that they are a bad influence in society.

It's a disturbing point. The media are all-pervasive. If there *are* problems, they must be very widespread. None of us will be unaffected by them.

So — *are* there problems?

A great many people seem to think that there are.

Media personality Malcolm Muggeridge, for example, sounds a note of doomsday.

'If it is the case, as I believe, that what we call Western civilization is fast distintegrating, then the media are playing a major role in the process.'

Christ and the Media, Hodder and Stoughton, 1977, p. 23.

Douglas Hurd, as Home Secretary, argued that television can influence people. 'I am afraid that there are some people, perhaps a small number . . . who are influenced in what they think and what they do by what they see on the box . . . Because I believe that happens, we have to take the subject seriously.'

Interview on *The World This Weekend,* September, 1987.

Journalist Robert Harris wrote a disturbing book about media coverage of the Falklands

11

Gotcha! The Media, the Government and the Falklands Crisis, Faber and Faber, 1983, p. 150.

War, claiming that the government and armed forces used the media as a propaganda machine. 'The Falklands conflict may well prove the last war in which the armed forces are completely able to control the movements and communications of the journalists covering it.'

Pressure groups, academics, media commentators, teachers and parents and many more, are arguing that there are things seriously wrong with the media, and that the effects upon us are harmful.

These are strong charges.

If they are true, then Christians should be taking a particular interest. Christians have a commitment to truth, to reality, to personal discipline, to social justice, and to the social, moral and spiritual welfare of the human race.

All of which are threatened by the media. Or so their critics claim.

So there is an urgent need to think biblically about the media. Do they really have power to influence us as well as to inform and entertain us? What should the function of the media be? What role should they play in our lives?

Telling the whole story

'If we can recognise, with American critic David Altheide, that "almost anything could be said about any event", then we should ask of any media text why that event or occasion was selected, why this or that way of treating it was chosen, and whose interests are served by amplifying, through reportage, its significance. Are there any events which have not been covered which might have provided a different perspective?'

Len Masterman, *Teaching the Media,* Comedia, 1985, p. 129.

Five key points for starters

In this book we're going to be talking particularly about soap operas, adverts and news stories. Its aim is to help us to get the best out of the media, and to think about them biblically just as we do about our choice of church, relationships, and which missionary society to support.

It's not an anti-media book. I like the media, and I hope you do too.

It's not one of those tranquil 'Meditations on the media' sort of books, either. This is an urgent matter. No Christian can opt out. I'll be giving some reasons why, as we go through the book.

It's not hard work. You don't need a university degree. And if we get to grips biblically with the media, our lives will be made richer.

Media wallpaper

There's no doubt that the media are among the most *pervasive* and *persuasive* phenomena of modern society.

They are part of the world we live in, part of the twentieth-century landscape. Like all landscapes that have grown familiar, we don't take much notice of them.

Every day, in countless ways, we experience them. We see newspaper headlines, listen to radio, watch television, and walk down streets displaying hoardings. To avoid the media, you would have to live a monastic life. To eliminate them entirely you would have to set up home on a desert island.

The total weekly media consumption of the average Briton has been estimated at 75 hours per week. Half of us listen to the radio every day, three quarters of us read a daily newspaper, and about 98% of British households possess one or more television sets.

Thousands of research projects have indicated that this massive presence in our lives has an effect; our lives are changed by the media.

Not all changes are for the worse. For example, the media have given extensive coverage to the issue of child sexual abuse. Esther Rantzen's television programmes, *Childline*, challenging advertisements, and major coverage by newspapers such as the *Daily Mail*

This is an urgent matter. No Christian can opt out . . . if we get to grips biblically with the media, our lives will be made richer.

have been seen by millions.

The result has been that many children have benefited, and some have been rescued from appalling situations of risk. Only the massive presence and influence of the media could have achieved such a result.

But the same power of persuasion can be — and often is — used in much less positive ways.

Media over-simplification

Issues in the media are often crudely compressed to the point of distortion.

If you were to read the newspapers, for example, you would think that most of the industrial unrest in Britain occurs in a small handful of industries.

By constantly reporting strikes at Ford, British Leyland, coal mines and hospitals, the Press implies that only a few industries are affected by industrial action.

But in reality the industries that the Press concentrate on aren't always the ones with the most problems.

Similarly, the constant emphasis on sex and violence might lead a visitor from another planet to conclude that these were the only moral problems mankind has. But of course there are many others.

Greed, intolerance, racism, stereotyping, and broken relationships are just some of the problems that we face today.

Partly because of the limitations of the media as communicators, and partly because of the commercial value of sex and violence in terms of sales and audiences, few of the other problems are ever properly discussed.

But many of them are widely reflected in the media.

For example, think of *Sons and Daughters,* a television soap opera which celebrates personal wealth and power, usually gained at the expense of relationships and elementary fairness.

Another example is the type of newspaper story which provides its readers with details of the private lives and squabbles of public figures. Well-known celebrities such as Joan Collins and Madonna have had much-publicized marriage problems. The gory details have been enthusiastically reported in the media.

Such stories have the superficial appeal of voyeurism, the readers being told intimate details of somebody else's private life. But their popularity really rests on the fascination that many people find in watching two people hurting each other.

There is also for many people the element of envy, and the gratification of discovering that money doesn't make other people happy.

Advertising can have a similar attraction. The appeal is often to greed, or pride, or selfishness. 'Go on — treat yourself,' says the alluring face; and visions of wonderful and unnecessary luxuries are dangled before you.

More is said than what is spoken

The media operate at a number of different levels, not all of which are obvious.

We will be looking at this fact in some detail in the next four chapters.

Like the face in which the lips smile but the eyes do not, the media can issue contradicting messages at the same time.

Page 3 of the *Sun* newspaper provides for its readers each day a photograph of a semi-nude woman. Although defenders of page 3 vigorously claim that it is all innocent fun, the text that goes with the picture is usually provocative and sexually teasing.

There is a clear invitation for male readers to fantasize about the girl in the photograph, and the newspaper collaborates in the fantasies. ('Feast your eyes on luscious Linda Lusardi . . . Mouth-watering, isn't she?')

Page 2, however, is reserved for the *Sun's* soapbox. There you will find moral indignation at government cuts, serious crime, world poverty . . . and sometimes, vicious rape.

The irony is strongest when a man convicted

of rape is said to have been addicted to pornography, which is likely to result in a headline 'SEX BEAST READ FILTH', or similar.

Two messages are being issued simultaneously here, and they conflict. One message is that drooling over half-naked women is fine provided the pictures are in a 'respectable family newspaper'; the other, that doing so if you then go out and rape somebody is quite a different matter.

I am not suggesting that page 3 of the *Sun* would lead somebody to rape. I do find it very inconsistent that 'filth' becomes 'fun' just because it's on a different page.

Putting things in their right context

One of the most interesting conclusions of current research into the media is that context is almost as important as content.

Some pressure groups, protesting about violence in the media, have complained about Tom and Jerry cartoons, on the grounds that they contain gratuitous violence. At the same time they have complained about films such as the *Rambo* series on the same grounds.

Yet there is a difference between the two. In *Tom and Jerry,* a character might be squashed flat, crushed into the ground, or have a hole drilled through him. But in the next frame he is back again, obviously completely unhurt.

Such cartoons are like the 'B' cowboy films in which everybody gets shot and nobody gets hurt.

The *Rambo* films and others of the same type are very different. There, death and wounding are highly believable. The weapons used are powerful and realistic, and those who are killed do not reappear, healthy or otherwise.

Because the two films are so different, the violence is a different kind of violence in each case.

You may disagree with my own opinion that Tom and Jerry cartoons are acceptable viewing; but I don't think that you can equate them with violent and ultra-realistic films.

For the same reason, there is only limited value in compiling lists of the number of times a particular swearword is used in a newspaper or in broadcasts.

An oath forced out of somebody who does not normally swear, in an situation of extreme distress, is something which a Christian will regret but should understand. It is quite different to the speech of a foul-mouthed blasphemer who can't complete a sentence without using obscenities or blasphemies. The two aren't the same.

What were you doing on the night J.R. was shot?

Another simplification often made about the media is to assume that we always experience them the same way.

But of course, we don't. Advertisers rely on this; they use the same images and slogans in newspapers, magazines, cinema, television, and street hoardings. Consequently we are exposed to the advertiser's message in many different places, when we are in many different states of mind.

And the chances of a successful persuasion to buy are increased.

Researchers into television viewing patterns placed cameras inside television sets, and the sets were installed into the homes of volunteer families. The families were then monitored as they watched.

The results showed that relatively little viewing was done by people sitting in front of the television, watching with undivided attention.

Most watched while something else was going on in the room. Some held conversations, some even read books and magazines. A few families were occupied in household tasks, homework and other distractions and were not facing the television at all.

These findings have had quite an impact on

> **We are exposed to the advertiser's message in many different places, when we are in many different states of mind.**

the 'effects debate', and have altered our understanding of how television influences us.

Similar factors apply to newspapers and magazines — something which is acknowledged by their owners, who publish a quite different newspaper for reading on the train in the morning from that which is read on a leisurely Sunday afternoon.

Paul's communication and ours

Read the following Bible passages, which all describe how Paul preached to, and talked, with unbelievers:

Acts 13:16-52; 17:16-34; 19:1-41; 28:17-31.

When Paul wanted to communicate with an audience that was not necessarily on his side, what methods did he use? How effective were they?

On that basis, how do you think Paul would have used today's media? (Do you think he *would* have used them?)

From these passages, can we draw some guidelines on

- Christian television channels, Christian cable TV, Christian-owned media (*e.g.* broadcasting stations, newspapers, advertising companies, *etc.*)?
- Christians working in the secular media?
- whether some media are more useful/ appropriate than others? (Are there any Paul would *not* have used?)
- presenting unbelievers with the gospel?

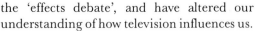

Putting it all together

So the media occupy a large part of our everyday lives.

Their influence extends into every area, and they communicate with us on many different levels.

For Christians, this poses problems. What is going to determine what we think and do?

- Is it going to be the media, with all their powers of persuasion?

● Or is it going to be what God is teaching us through prayer, the Bible, and the help of other Christians?

We can't be complacent. Let me repeat, it's an urgent matter. The media aren't in business to make us better Christians. If we don't work out *as Christians* how the media should fit into our lives, they will probably make us worse ones!

If we want to be powerful ambassadors for Christ in a world which largely doesn't want to know, it's *essential* that we understand about the power and influence of the media.

If we want to grow as Christians, it's *vital* that we make Jesus Lord of *everything* — of *EastEnders* as well as *Songs of Fellowship,* of the *Daily Mirror* as well as *Strait* and *21st Century Christian,* of Radio 1 as well as Greenbelt and Spring Harvest.

There can't be any no-go areas for Jesus.

Least of all in the media.

It isn't a soft option. It isn't really an 'option' at all — we have no choice. If we live in this century, it's something which as Christians we *have* to think about.

Which doesn't mean that we have to give the media up. As we'll see, we can actually enjoy them more.

As we'll find in the next chapter, where we are talking soap operas.

chapter two

TV soap opera – windowing the world

Wacky, charming Clive Gibbons (but there was always a troubled look in those crinkly eyes) finally comes clean and tells his brother why he quit medicine.

Once he had a glittering career as a doctor ahead of him. Then his girlfriend telephoned him at the hospital. She had a blinding headache. Could he help? But he was busy and told her to take a couple of aspirin. Later that night she died of a massive stroke. Heartbroken and racked by guilt, Clive gave up medicine for ever.

While his brother is sympathizing, Lucy, a neighbour's child, finds a picture of the dead girl. Clive tells her it is a picture of a very special friend. At that moment, the doorbell rings. 'Clive!' Lucy shouts, *It's the girl in the photograph!'*

As the music swells, the closing credits roll up the screen. Another episode of *Neighbours* has come to an end.

Of course you'll be watching when the next episode is screened. Who wouldn't be? And if you're a regular viewer, you'll be only slightly disappointed to learn that Clive's girlfriend really did die, and that this is not her ghost at the door. No, it's her beautiful sister Louise.

Will Clive fall in love with her? Will Louise replace the lost great love of his life? And would it work anyway?

For the answers, tune into the next episode. And after that there'll be other crises and other episodes and other crises and other episodes . . .

The British spend 80 million man-hours a week watching TV soap opera — which is longer than it took mediaeval man to build a cathedral.

Ted Harrison, *Soundings,* Radio 4, 1985.

The soap bubble

Soap opera is big business.

The first soaps were American radio programmes funded by the soap manufacturers in the 1930s, aimed at a housewife audience.

Today, soap operas have audiences of millions. *EastEnders* is watched by over one-third of the British population, and we spend 80 million man-hours each week watching TV soap opera.

On the three major American TV networks, there are 11 hours of soap opera screened each weekday. The daily audience is 35 million.

Missing an episode can be such a catastrophe that in Britain some newspapers run weekly columns updating readers on soap plot developments, and in American Greyhound bus stations you can watch recent soap opera episodes on video machines in the waiting area.

Christians and soap opera

For a great many Christians, soap opera has been a considerable problem.

Most obviously, it devours time. TV is a problem for anyone wanting to be responsible in their use of time, but soap is doubly so. A committed soap addict will build the week around the soaps, making certain to be in front of a TV when they are transmitted.

Even a moderate viewer will have to make some decisions. Is there a right balance between watching TV and other activities? How does it affect our priorities?

These are important questions.

They are not the only issues raised by soap opera. But they are probably the easiest to identify.

The use of time, and how we set our priorities, are problems that are not unique to TV. There is ample guidance in the Bible on these matters, and what is said there applies as much to TV as to anything else.

'Time Management' is rapidly becoming a

new religion in management circles. There is an increasing number of books by Christians on the same subject. Most people would find it helpful, whatever work they do, occasionally to make a checklist of just how their time is being divided up.

Doing so will indicate whether or not the place of TV in our scale of priorities needs rethinking.

Other issues can't be identified so easily. How, for example, do the interests and concerns of soap opera relate to those of the Bible? Is there any incompatibility between being a Christian and watching soap opera?

Getting under the lather

It's been a lousy bus ride home, the weather's atrocious, and what we most want to do is to grab something to eat and collapse in front of the TV.

So we fix ourselves some bread and cheese, make a cup of coffee, and curl up gratefully in front of the set.

At times like this the TV is a faithful standby. We can catch up on the day's events. Dip into a soap opera for half an hour. See whether the latest hopeful has dethroned Steve Davies in the snooker.

You know where you are with television . . . it puts up pictures on the screen and you watch them . . . a manageable, easily handled source of news and entertainment that doesn't make demands on you.

Or is it?

Like all the media, TV is not such a simple means of communication as it first appears.

When we watch a news report, for example, we may think we are watching an individual telling us the facts of a particular situation, that we are being told what actually happened.

But we are not. We are certainly being given information, but *in a particular way* (in chapter four we will be examining how this works).

And that will affect how we understand what

TV is showing us.

Soap opera works the same way. It is an image with many surfaces. It is a story with many meanings. Some of those meanings, of course, are contained in what the characters actually *say* to each other, but some are assumptions, never actually spelt out but *implied* in the way the programme is made.

TV soap opera is a popular and powerful medium of entertainment. As a nation we watch a great deal of it. But even if we ration our viewing, it's important to be aware that, once again, much more is being said than what is actually being spoken.

Neighbours

In the opening credits of *Neighbours,* a number of things are communicated to us about the story and its characters. Here are a few:

- These are close-knit families (shown by facial expressions, comradely gestures, having fun together).

- This is a small, self-contained community (the credits include a map).

- You are going to enjoy this programme because it is about having fun and meeting fun people (a window is broken and everybody laughs).

- This is a world where life is generally happy and peaceful (the colours are all pastel, warm tones, no stark contrasts; and the signature tune is lilting and dance-like).

Watch the credits of your favourite TV programme and do a checklist of how many things are said — before a word is even spoken.

'The medium is the message'

As Marshall McLuhan pointed out in the sixties, the medium *is* the message. *What* is said is reinforced — or sometimes, contradicted — by *how* it is said. The media influence us explicitly — and implicitly.

One way soap opera can affect the way we think is through the various 'models' it offers us.

Soap opera presents various views of what success is, what makes people happy, how we should treat one another, what are the things that give us dignity and self-worth, and so on.

> **Soap operas present various views of success, happiness, what gives us dignity and self-worth and how people should treat others.**

The characters themselves rarely express such views in words. But the statement is made by the props, the backgrounds, the things people respect in the soap and what they despise.

Unspoken values and assumptions can add up to a very explicit statement. And if we watch a soap regularly, it's easy to adopt its assumptions unconsciously.

Does this mean that we should never watch soap opera? Isn't it dangerous to open ourselves to something which is influencing us in subtle and indirect ways?

I don't think it is, necessarily. But it means that we have to be careful. We need to be sure that *we*, rather than TV, are choosing what our enjoyment is going to be based upon.

To illustrate this let's look at one particular model — the family. What, in the world of soap opera, *is* a family?

There are a number of different models to choose from. Let me identify four.

Home is where the hate is

First, the family presented as a network of frictions and problems.

In many soap operas, families are the arenas for feuding, rivalry and unhappiness.

A typical example on British TV is the Australian soap, *Sons and Daughters*. The (highly complex) plot involves marriage, divorce, children siding with one parent against another, contested legacies and disputed real estate. It seems that to be born into a family (whether you're a Hamilton, a Morrell or a Thompson) means to be forced to take sides in numerous conflicts.

By and large, in *Sons and Daughters* tenderness and family affection are means of affirming one family's solidarity against another. Younger members are recruited by older members for their cause, and everybody has a wonderfully vindictive time.

No place like home

Secondly, the family presented as a warm, romantic, ideal picture from the past.

This quite different model comes in soaps such as *The Waltons*, *Neighbours* and *The Sullivans*. Here the family is presented as a symbol of traditional values, usually representing a span of several generations.

The old pass on their wisdom and their values to the young. The young bring joy to their parents, struggle with the various crises of growing up, and from time to time impart their own wisdom to their elders.

Often such families live in environments that are themselves rooted in the past. Sometimes the soap is explicitly old-fashioned (the Sullivans, for example, are an Australian wartime family). Sometimes, as in *Coronation Street,* what seems an authentic portrayal of contemporary life really reflects a community and a lifestyle that vanished long ago (if they ever existed at all).

In either case, family membership here means being part of a supportive, caring, committed group of people, who stand firm against just about everything life can throw at them.

First families

Yet another family model appears in soaps such as *Dynasty* and *Dallas*: the family as dynasty. Here the family has an importance much greater than its individual members.

There are thirteen different soap operas running on British television. Of these, nine are based on the lives of fictional families.

To be born a Ewing in Dallas is to be like royalty. And when two family dynasties clash, the consequences affect thousands of lives. Families like these are usually dominated by the figure of their founder (such as 'Daddy' in *Dallas*). Members wishing to justify their actions often appeal to his memory.

The dynastic family is also an arena for conflict, but the conflicts are usually over how best to ensure the survival of the dynasty. The conflicts are presided over by the older members of the family, who stand aloof from the nitty-gritty of the battlefield.

An interesting variant is *Neighbours*. To be one of the Ramseys of Ramsey Street is not the social asset it once was (Max, who boasts of it, is gently ridiculed). But Helen, grandmother to the Robinson family, fills the role of wise matriarch of the Robinson dynasty.

Family fortunes

Finally, there is a model of the family which is found in many soaps: the family as achiever and possessor.

In *Brookside*, for example, ownership of a house in the private housing estate symbolizes family success. In American soaps, family togetherness is often presented against a backdrop of a large swimming pool and several expensive cars. Storylines in *Coronation Street* have made home ownership a highly desirable target for families to aim at.

A subtle variant of this is the flawless physical perfection often found in soap characters. How often do you see an ugly, fat, short or disabled person given sympathetic treatment in a soap opera?

In *Dallas*, *Dynasty* and many more, everybody in the family has that healthy, glowing, handsome perfection which only money can provide.

Choosing between models

It's important that we should be aware that different kinds of models are being presented

> **How often do you see an ugly, fat, short or disabled person given sympathetic treatment in a soap opera?**

to us. But it's also important that we should avoid oversimplified responses.

Christians should reject the model of the family as a network of frictions; not all families are unhappy, and unhappiness is not part of the biblical norm for families.

But that doesn't mean that we should automatically opt for the second model, the family as an ideal from the past.

Family life today is, for many people, far from the romantic ideal of Walton Mountain. Many Christians and non-Christians live in families that are not supportive, and many Christian families struggle with poverty, sickness, unemployment and other burdens.

The third and fourth models (dynastic and materialistic families) are easier to handle, because clearer biblical guidelines are involved. But it's still important to avoid simplistic reactions.

Some Christians have suggested there should be 'Christian soap operas', in an attempt to exploit the enormous popular appeal of such programmes. But often what they are really asking for is a Christian *Waltons* or *A Country Practice* where Christian faith and life would be expressed by a tranquil rural life.

Real Christianity does not deal with Hollywood ideals or all-year-round suntan at all. Which is why many imported (and a few home-grown) soaps consistently fail to make contact with the world as it really is.

> **Christians should reject the model of the family as a network of frictions; unhappiness is not part of the biblical norm for families.**

Don't scrub soap

I am not suggesting that we should cut soap opera out of our lives. Here are just three reasons.

Good entertainment

Many soaps hold their huge audiences by sheer skill. All of them know how to generate compulsive storylines. Some (such as *Coronation Street*) have gifted actors.

For such reasons, soap has a valid place in

> **Soap is a 'cultural indicator' — if we understand its appeal, we will understand our fellow human beings better.**

popular entertainment comparable to the popular novel of earlier times.

Social significance

Soap is of absorbing interest to many millions of our neighbours. It's worth pondering what it is that makes it so compelling.

Soap is a 'cultural indicator' — if we understand its appeal, we will understand our fellow human beings better.

Which is something Christians should be seeking to do.

Moral relevance

Soap has a valuable role in our society as an *advocate*. It involves viewers in moral and ethical choices.

When J. R. Ewing was shot in *Dallas*, 21 million people in Britain argued over whether the shooting was morally justified. In a society which has turned away from Christianity, soap opera is for many people a rare opportunity to practise ethics — to think hard about moral issues.

Some soaps, such as *Brookside* and *EastEnders*, have dealt very responsibly with issues such as unmarried motherhood and rape.

Soap — and flannel

While soap opera can have real excellence, however, it can also present major problems for Christians (and, indeed for any thoughtful viewer).

The fodder factor

Soap opera offers, to a society that has largely discarded religion, a fantasy in which God is almost always irrelevant. In the world of soap, people achieve happiness through their own or others' efforts.

Millions of lonely, unemployed, or simply bored people watch soap endlessly. No wonder; it offers the opportunity to slip for a while into a dream world, in which such problems rarely appear.

This is true of certain American and Australian (especially daytime) soaps. The British realist tradition of *Brookside* and *EastEnders* is much more open to such issues. But for millions, soap opera is a solace, a comfort, a flight from reality.

But Christians believe that there really *are* answers to human social and spiritual needs.

The fudge factor

In many soaps (a good example is *Neighbours*) moral issues are raised only to be trivialized. But there is an even more disturbing aspect of this 'moral fudging'. Very often, soap's immense persuasive powers are used to raise an issue in order silently to influence viewers' opinions on it.

For example, in *EastEnders,* a long-running storyline involved two male homosexuals living together. This storyline has been used to promote some balanced teaching on AIDS ('You can't get it by shaking hands', *etc.*). Explicit sex between the couple, and bedroom scenes, are never portrayed. (*Brookside*, which also has a homosexual subplot, permits rather more open expression of affection.)

Yet, the storyline carries a very strong silent message. It aims at 'positive representation' of homosexuality. Anybody who treats homosexuality as anything less than totally acceptable is criticized or ridiculed in *EastEnders*. 'Christian' comment is put in the mouth of middle-aged Dot Cotton, who is portrayed as a dithering harmless busybody. Disquiet about homosexual practices is dismissed as moral prejudice.

This is not a discussion. It is a campaign. We watch, but we are being influenced towards an opinion.

To complicate matters, for a long time one of the partners was under the legal age for sex between consenting males. But there clearly was a sexual relationship (at one stage the police took a great interest in the couple). So advocacy of liberal views of sex ends up endorsement of illegal sex.

This abuse of the power of the media should at the very least provoke a demand that the programme be rescheduled. At present it goes out at 7.30 p.m., which is firmly within accepted 'family viewing hours'.

The frivolity factor

So should Christians spend time watching soap opera?

Those most opposed to TV say 'No.' They argue that soap opera wastes time, is irrelevant to the gospel, and promotes secular, unbiblical values. They point to soaps like *EastEnders* and ask how any Christian could find them entertaining.

Much of this is valid. Some soaps, for example, have most of the bad points we have been considering, and very few of the good ones. They seem to be fairly mindless entertainment. Some Christians refuse to watch them, and they have good reasons for their choice.

Making up our minds

So there are arguments for and against soaps. On which side should we come down?

I believe that there is a place for soap opera in the life of any Christian who is interested in the world and culture in which he or she lives, though the amount of time devoted to it will be a matter for each person carefully to decide.

Soaps are enjoyed and followed by millions.

Anybody at all interested in sharing the gospel ought to have at least *some* knowledge of what it is that most people find so interesting.

Yet there are better reasons for watching soap, and we have looked at some of them in passing.

- The best soap *is good entertainment* and can be justified in the same way that occasionally reading a popular novel can be justified. (Of course, if you read novels for two hours every day there would be a problem!)
- Soap *can make us think critically and intelligently* about the world we live in. It is common ground not only between people of one country, but between people across the globe.
- Soap *raises questions* that people are asking today. Too often the church has had the

answers but has not known what the questions are.

So yes, for many of us soap opera will be a good and enjoyable thing to watch, and we will all have different reasons.

Perhaps we will watch in order to understand people better, and to understand one of the most powerful contemporary idols. Perhaps soap will become part of our entertainment, to be used with care and enjoyed for what it offers.

But it can never be something we watch entirely uncritically. That doesn't mean we have to sit on the edge of our seats, watching anxiously for the first deviation from an orthodox biblical world-view.

It does mean that we must keep part of ourselves detached, so that we don't surrender ourselves to the experience and submit to whatever the makers of the programme wish to say to us.

We need a balance.

On the one hand the creativity of the programme-maker must be allowed to intrigue,

A Good Soap Guide

Check out the soap you watch with this quick checklist:

● Are families portrayed as
   A. Something to be endured,
   B. Something to be enjoyed,
   C. Something to be exploited?

● What is its view of the future?
   A. The future is going to be wonderful — at least for us.
   B. If we all work hard the future could be really good.
   C. Who cares about the future when you're having fun today?

absorb and sometimes captivate us, whether it be an award-winning series like *The Jewel in the Crown* or a down-market, low-budget soap opera like *Santa Barbara*. (You never heard of that one? You haven't missed a great deal.)

On the other hand, we must not set our Christian commitment and critical perceptions to one side as we watch soap opera. We are as much Christians when we watch TV as when we attend church.

Striving for that balance isn't easy, but it isn't a burden. It isn't a shackling of our liberty. It's part of our Christian freedom to be truly human in the world that God has made.

Yet the final note has to be one of caution. We are truly free only when we acknowledge that God and his moral character are sovereign over *everything*. If we allow soap opera and TV to occupy a part of our lives separate from our lives as Christians, we will find that we are hooked after all!

We are as much Christians when we watch TV as when we attend church.

- What is the place of God in the soap?
  A. Not mentioned — not really necessary.
  B. Some people seem to take him seriously but most of us aren't sure.
  C. If he really existed he wouldn't want to know us anyway.

Three A's: This soap is probably not rotting your soul, but it's not going to turn you into a spiritual giant. **Three B's:** This soap is at least in contact with real people and might make you think a bit. **Three C's:** This one probably won't rot your soul either, but do you really need all that cynicism twice a week?

chapter three

Unmasking adverts

We're bombarded by adverts. Wherever we go, we are invited to spend. We are shown pictures of desirable goods and services, and we are given reasons why we're entitled to have them. On your way to the Oxfam shop you will pass hundreds of invitations to spoil yourself. Give yourself that little extra; you deserve it.

We're encouraged to want more than we need. Adverts entice us, give us glimpses into a world of luxury.

We see the kind of people we would like to become. People who are dressed as we would like to dress. People who live in houses we envy. People who have things we can't afford.

Even their bread rises properly. Their whites wash brighter than ours. Their batteries last longer. Their slimming works. Their airline looks after them and treats them like royalty.

The key to entry into this privileged world?

Buy the product. Use the service. Take advantage of the special offer. Buy now.

Whatever is a Christian to make of all this?

Adverts — a daily diet

Breakfast: 1 advert on cornflake packet
1 advert on bread wrapper
2 pieces of junk mail (1 life-insurance flier, 1 film-processing offer)
35 minutes Radio 1 (ads for other programmes, Radio 1 offers)
10 minutes TV-AM (while getting dressed)

Several 20ft-high posters on street hoardings
Front page of somebody else's newspaper (on the bus)
Adverts on somebody's ghettoblaster (Capital Radio)

At college: total of 1 hour miscellaneous Radio 1
Adverts in Common Room (student travel, cheap insurance, bank with the listening bank and get a snappy cheque-book cover)
Magazines — *Time Out, NME,* and others
Adverts and miscellaneous street radio noises going home.

Home: Commercial radio till supper
Adverts on food packets. Special offer on coffee jar
BBC ads for programmes later tonight
Brookside with commercials before, during and after
Radio 1 till bed . . .

What — me influenced?

Most of us would claim that adverts don't affect us unduly. We would say that an advert is an attempt by those marketing a product to present it in the most attractive light. We then make a more or less considered decision. Do we need or want the object or service being advertised?

Many adverts, we would say, don't affect us at all. We simply don't notice them. The advertisers have failed by over-exposure.

But that is not how the advertising industry sees it at all. Advertisers talk about you and me as 'targets'. They tailor their work very specifically for particular targets. They know which audiences are susceptible to their product.

When TV sells advertising space, it is selling audiences. It is selling you and me.

It offers advertisers a known audience to which to advertise. The fee is fixed according to what kind of an audience it is. If a programme is watched by a predominantly prosperous audience ranging in age from early twenties to late forties, it will cost more to advertise in its commercial breaks than in a programme aimed at older people, who are known to spend less.

So when we see an advert on TV, it is there because the advertisers knew we would be watching it!

The same is true of advertising in newspapers. Different adverts appear in different newspapers. The potential audience is taken into account.

> **When TV sells advertising space, it is selling audiences. It is selling you and me.**

'Hidden persuaders'

But advertisers do not simply identify audiences in order to expose them to the qualities of the goods they wish to sell.

Adverts actually manipulate the audience. And they do it in a number of ways. The manipulation is almost never perceived by those who experience it. This is what Vance Packard meant when he coined the phrase, 'hidden persuaders'.

Be one of the in-crowd

One way that many adverts exert an appeal is to suggest that if you buy the product or service, you will be accepted and welcomed by your colleagues, your contemporaries — your 'peer group'.

So we're invited to join the Pepsi generation, to go on safari holidays with our own age-group, or to buy some item of clothing which will identify us as members of a group.

Adverts like these use an armoury of techniques to emphasize their message. The group of young people embarking on the expensive holiday is physically close. They have their arms around each other. They are smiling and waving. Nobody is on the fringe, everybody is accepted in the group. Nobody is lonely.

Similar results are achieved by the broad camera angle and choral singing in the Pepsi-Cola adverts. A predominantly young choir sings about unity and hope. The well-known soft-drink label is linked with hopes for a peaceful future. The event has an almost religious aura.

On the surface, such adverts are attractive statements about the cost and features of what is being advertised.

But more is being said, much more powerfully, though without words. If you will only buy our product, you will get much more for your money. Acceptance . . . happiness . . . even (for the price of a soft drink) a future for the world.

Follow the yellowbrick road

Advertising today speaks to a society in which many people have less than they need. There is widespread unemployment. There is social insecurity. There are enormous urban problems. There is a growing economic inequality between north and south, both nationally and globally.

Much advertising is addressed to people's insecurity and fears. For example, more than one advert paints a picture of the future. Mr and Mrs Consumer are relaxing at home. They look healthy and prosperous. Clearly they are enjoying a comfortable and pleasurable retirement, the fruit of wise financial planning.

These adverts are produced by investment and insurance companies. At the most accessible level they are selling policies and unit trusts. But at a deeper level, they are selling the future. Peace of mind and personal security, they suggest, are not only within reach. They are available at reasonable prices.

A version of this is a feature of British Telecom's telephone adverts. They imply that having a telephone will ensure that your old age (or your student years, or your life in Australia) will not lack loving and regular communications with your relatives.

Take the waiting out of wanting

Of course, a great deal of advertising appeals to our desire to have more than we already have. We are shown images of plenty. You can have it *now*.

Advertising like this has two main thrusts. It attempts to make us discontented with what we already have. And it attempts to show us that we can have more with very little effort.

The first aim, that of making us discontented, is achieved by glamorous illustrations and seductive words.

'Happiness . . . Happiness . . . with the boat that we possess,' croons the voice-over, while we see a screen shot of a moored yacht on a coastline that looks as if it came straight out of a James Bond movie.

Invest with the advertiser, it's implied, and you too can enter the glamorous, moneyed life with all that ownership of a yacht implies.

This is advertising by association, and many adverts do it. For example, an upmarket mail-order catalogue is advertised with a picture of

> **" . . . it attempts to make us discontented with what we already have . . . and to show us that we can have more with very little effort. "**

a family sitting on an expensive sofa. The room has expensive wallpaper, old leather-bound books, fine prints, choice pottery. The father is telephoning. He is ordering from the catalogue.

Here is a family, it's implied, that is used to the good things in life. They have taste, sophistication, leisure and money. People like that order from our catalogue; so can you. Enter into their world, by shopping from their catalogue.

Have you got the message?

Look at this advert.
- What is it trying to sell you?
- What advantage does it say you will gain if you purchase?
- Does the picture back this up? Are there any implied advantages in the picture that aren't mentioned in the words?
- What is the advert really saying about possessions/people/wealth?

The second aim — that of offering more return for less money — is achieved by drawing attention to massive price reductions and/or easy finance. '£50 off now' . . . 'Interest-free credit' . . . 'Prices must rise on December 1st' . . . 'Special offer for a limited period'.

In adverts aimed at the less well-off, it's often implied that thrifty, responsible people should buy the product. 'It's not only glamorous,' we're told, 'It can actually be *cheaper* to buy this than your normal brand.'

For example, in some adverts glamorous celebrities appear in supermarkets. They confront housewives with a choice of product. Then they reveal that the one they opted for on grounds of pleasure/taste/effectiveness was in fact the most economical/familiar.

Gentlemen, start your engines.

For a very special kind of person . . .

A common implication of advertising is that if you buy the product or service, you will reach a new and higher status.

Some credit cards are advertised like that. Potential purchasers are asked whether they are among the select few who will be granted this special spending power. (In reality, obtaining one is relatively easy.)

Many products and services are advertised with the implication that ownership will tell the world you've made it, you're an in-person.

But it's an illusory image. The adverts appear in the mass media. Hundreds of thousands of the 'ordinary public' must be eligible to purchase what is on offer. That is why, for example, few of the 'collectors' items' advertised in the Sunday supplements ever will become genuinely desirable rarities. 'I don't wish to join,' said Groucho Marx, 'a club that would have me for a member.'

But the adverts succeed because the 'hook' is entry into a select circle. The lure is strong. You will be accepted among porcelain-plate collectors, credit-card shoppers, owners of leather-bound filing systems, and many more. A great many people find that hard to resist.

What a friend we have in ... Volkswagen

Some adverts attach absolute moral values to what they sell.

A series of TV adverts for Volkswagen cars, for example, make the VW a symbol of dependability.

It's not simply reliability and low repair bills, though that is the primary meaning of the adverts.

They contain images of betrayal, of loss, of human folly and recklessness. In a world which has suddenly proved faithless, the Volkswagen provest trustworthy. It never lets you down. It is a steadfast friend.

The image is reinforced by the lyrics: 'Everyone is going through changes . . .', set to the tune of 'What a friend we have in Jesus'. The allusion will be picked up by thousands who are not Christians but remember Sunday School.

In the same way, a series of brilliant adverts for Oxo cubes does much more than establish the food qualities of the product. Stews and casseroles become the symbols of family unity. A simmering Oxo-flavoured hotpot can mend family rifts. Disconsolate and irritable teenagers become transformed characters when Mum puts the soup on the table. Everybody lends a hand when Oxo is on the menu.

These are a few of the ways in which advertising shapes how we see a product. There are many more.

Techniques of the soft sell

How does advertising achieve its powerful effects? How are we so easily influenced?

Advertising is a unique form of communication. It short-cuts many of the usual ways of receiving information.

Many adverts do not even need the product to be included. Everybody knows what is being talked about. Others rely on simple visual clues, like the Silk Cut cigarette campaign which uses no words at all, just photographs of pieces of silk with cuts in them.

The techniques of film and video are used heavily. TV and cinema adverts have often cost as much to produce as a small feature film. The message is conveyed by image. Words are secondary.

In fact, advertising is much more of a code than a language. Words are used in compressed and witty ways. What seems to have only one meaning turns out to have several. The target audience willingly attempts to decode the message.

When the *Financial Times* advertises with the slogan, 'No *FT* — no comment', we spend time working out what it means. We are actually helping the advertiser to advertise to us!

The drip effect

This is why adverts that feature products and services we already know about still have the power to influence us.

> **. . . more of a code than a language . . . audiences attempt to work out the message.**

We know about Heineken lager. We know it exists because we have seen hundreds of adverts for it. But the latest variant on 'refreshing the parts other beers can't reach' can still amuse us. We spend a few moments working it out, decoding it.

And for those few moments the product is being reinforced in our minds.

Taking the message on board

Usually, we don't even realize we are decoding the advert. We think we are dealing with a simple statement. We aren't aware of the many layers of meaning. Just as in soap opera, we are hearing more than we are listening to.

Reinforcement On the simplest level, advertising works as reinforcement.

An example is the frequent use of puns in advertising. Double meanings, word plays and deliberate misquotations make the same point in many different ways, and each time, we're interested.

The Heineken campaign mentioned earlier is based on endless variations of 'Refreshes the parts other beers can't reach' — bad Heineken

verbal puns have included a poet looking for inspiration ('refreshes the *poets* other beers can't reach').

The same technique with pictures instead of words has produced British Telecom's *Yellow Pages* slogan ('Let your fingers do the walking'), and the Benson and Hedges cigarette adverts which use the shape and colour of the package in a variety of bizarre settings.

Hidden meanings At a more complicated level, the various meanings differ from each other For example, a simple statement about the desirability of luxury goods can conceal sexist messages, conveyed by the images the advert uses.

Many perfumes, furs and cosmetics are advertised with an underlying image of male mastery. The handsome man in the background is pleased his woman looks so good because he owns the woman. She is his property, his plaything. The image is reinforced in subtle ways. The meaning may not be instantly read, but it is there.

It exists at many levels. The Cadbury's campaign featuring the 'All because the lady loves Milk Tray' theme is superficially about female mastery. A superbly fit, handsome hero undergoes incredible risk and exertion simply to deliver a box of chocolates to a woman.

But in fact it is highly patronising. It portrays women as beautiful dolls, with infantile whims. The heroic superman gives her the chocolates she wants because he feels like doing so. The advert reminds us of a kindly uncle giving in to a fretful child.

A Woolworths promotional leaflet advertised Christmas toys. All the boys' toys were on one double-page spread. They featured guns, construction sets, and activity toys. The girls' spread featured dolls, housekeeping toys, and fluffy 'huggable' toys.

The hidden message was reinforced by the use of colour — strong, dramatic greens, reds and khaki for the boys; soft pastel shades for the girls.

The imagery upheld stereotypes which were certainly not the primary message of the advert.

But the stereotypes played a major part in reinforcing the product's appeal.

Chapter and verse

There is nothing in the Bible that speaks about advertising. (Advertising as we know it is usually thought to have originated in Elizabethan times.)

But we are told a great deal about resisting the pressures of the world. Many Bible writers urge us not to allow our minds to be manipulated. And we are given a number of illustrations of what our lives should be like. We're shown what our hopes, ambitions and material expectations should be.

These are basic issues when we think about advertising.

A mixed blessing

Advertising has brought many benefits to mankind. Reform, welfare, aid, health campaigns, charity appeals and many other good things have been made easier by advertising.

But there are also many problems.

In its manipulation of people, much advertising keeps a variety of social evils and injustices in existence.

Built-in obsolescence ensures that products have a shorter life than necessary, so maintaining demand. This advertisers' device wastes scarce resources.

There are 800 million hungry people in this world. In our own country, many have nowhere to live, no job to do, and no way of providing basic needs for their families.

Yet adverts encourage us to long for second homes, second cars, and personal wealth. They encourage us to hog the world's resources for ourselves.

While Mr and Mrs Western are choosing between Ibiza and the Greek Islands for their 'winter break', in underdeveloped countries people walk along streets that stink of human excrement, scavenging for food.

These are a few of the social evils that advertising can make worse. There are many more.

Biblical challenges to lifestyle

Don't long for wealth

The biblical picture of the Christian life is one of contentment, not desire for luxury. The people of God are often blessed with prosperity, but the overriding theme is not material wealth but responsibility before God as to how you use it.

'I know what it is to be in need,' says Paul, 'and I know what it is to have plenty. I have learned the secret of being content . . .' (*Philippians 4 12*).

Jesus talked about personal wealth and its spiritual implications: 'Where your treasure is, there your heart will be also' (*Matthew 6:21*).

Advertising tells us that we should desire what we don't need. The Bible's teaching, so

> **I know what it is to be in need, and I know what it is to have plenty. I have learned the secret of being content.**
>
> Paul, *Philippians 4:12*

far as material possessions are concerned, is summed up by Paul. 'My God will meet all your needs according to his glorious riches in Christ Jesus' (*Philippians 4:19*).

Wealth in human terms, however, is never without danger: 'You say, "I am rich; I have acquired wealth and do not need a thing." But you do not realise that you are wretched, pitiful, poor, blind and naked' (*Revelation 3:17*).

Have Jesus' attitude to possessions

Christians should have 'renewed minds'. (The same Greek word is used in *Romans 12:2* and *Ephesians 4:23*.) Our renewed mind should be the mind of Christ (*1 Corinthians 2:16*).

What did Jesus think about wealth and possessions?

He was at ease with the rich and the poor alike. But he acknowledged that wealth was a handicap, rather than an advantage.

Wealth hinders people from realizing that human beings have deep spiritual needs. When you can afford to have things just as you want them, you don't look to God for help — and you become selfish.

Wealth means that charity becomes painless. Rich people sometimes think they can buy their way into heaven. But Jesus pointed out that a fully laden camel could pass through the cramped Needle Gateway more easily than a rich person could get into heaven (*Matthew 19:24; Mark 10:25; Luke 18:25*).

Don't be manipulated

Jesus had an analytical mind. He saw beneath the surface of things. He never gave pat answers to questions. His answers showed that he understood the underlying question that the questioner really wanted to ask.

He refused to be manipulated. Politicians and pressure groups tried to use him and trick him. He declined.

Living with adverts means taking them seriously. We should take time to look at some of them closely. How are they attempting to manipulate? What 'hooks' are they using? What assumptions do they ask us to accept? Do they appeal to good instincts in us, or selfish ones? Most adverts offer to change our lives in some way or other — but into what?

Paul repeatedly warns against following fashionable trends, often quite strongly (*e.g. 1 Corinthians 6:17 ff.*). And he urges us not to be pressurized or exploited. In a very important passage, he says: 'Don't let the world around you squeeze you into its own mould, but let God remould your minds from within' (*Romans 12:2, J. B. Phillips' translation*).

Realistically, we can never be entirely free from the pressures of advertising. Many of us buy particular products because adverts have persuaded us to.

But we *can* develop a critical and independent mind, so that resisting the pressures and manipulations of advertising becomes part of our normal thinking.

We can — and we should. If we don't, we are not following Jesus, and we're certainly not becoming like him.

> **We can never be entirely free from the pressures of advertising ... but we *can* develop a critical and independent mind.**

chapter four

The news media – telling the truth

As I write this chapter, a dog is in the news.

It is an expert skier. Two paws strapped to each ski, it glides down the slopes. It also swims and dives. Goggled underwater, it glides around like a canine Jacques Costeau.

But what has made the dog a media celebrity is that it has also learned to water-ski. So now it is on TV, riding the waves, holding on to a rope for dear life as it follows a speedboat out across the water.

It's a 'silly season' story, one of those pieces of whimsy which are chosen to round off the broadcast news.

But it illustrates some characteristics of the news media.

It's the way we tell 'em

In the Radio 1 *Newsbeat* office, at the *News at Ten* editorial desk, in the offices of the *Daily Mail,* and in news departments all over the world, the news is piling up.

As you read this book, reports are arriving from news agencies: stories that are just breaking, updates of yesterday's news, pictures coming in by wire. Some material is coming in by satellite link. Correspondents and reporters are sending their copy by telephone and cable. Faxes and telexes, couriers and newsfilm agencies are all playing their part in producing an avalanche of information.

Decisions are being made. Some news will

have to be gathered specially. For major stories reporters and camera teams will have to be sent out. For others, agencies will be used. How much should be spent? Does the story justify the cost of reporting it?

Meanwhile, the clock moves relentlessly on.

Out of the mass of information, the day's 'news' has to be selected.

When the choice of *what* is to be used is made, the choice of *how* it will be used must be made.

In the *Newsbeat* office, decisions are being made on how to share out the precious fifteen minutes. What will be the main story? What will be broadcast as a tail-end piece? Should the political story have more space than the rock revelation?

In the *News at Ten* office, reports have come in of a row in the House of Commons. Should a political commentator be called into the studio to talk about it? Does it merit a live interview with a government spokesman? If so, should the opposition spokesman be invited to speak as well?

In the newspaper office similar decisions are being made. Should a Royal story, with its stunning photos, go on the front page? Or should an industrial story be featured?

What will be given major coverage — extended interviews, double page spread, extensive archive footage? What will get half an inch on an inside page? And what will have to be left out altogether?

In a courtroom drama, it's revealed that Frankie Goes to Hollywood's two major chart successes were performed almost entirely by synthesizers. Is that news? If it is, is it front-page news? Is it more important than an old lady being mugged? And what story has to be dropped to make room for it?

Such decisions are crucial if the news is to be at all interesting. But news editing involves assumptions about relevance, importance, and values. It influences us in the response we make to the news.

> **From information to 'news': *what* is to be used and *how* is it to be used?**

It arranges items in an order of importance, and in so doing, it interprets as it reports. If you go into any newsagent and look at the day's newspapers, you will see a wide range of opinions as to what the main news of the day is. The *Sun* and *The Times* will have made different choices.

It depends what you call 'news'

For tabloids like the *Daily Mirror* and the *Star*, 'news' can mean Princess Di rather than Arthur Scargill.

When Mr Scargill resigned as NUM president to stand for re-election, the story was crammed into a small corner of the front page of the *Daily Mirror*.

The lead story featured Princess Diana's schooldays ('NAUGHTY NAUGHTY — WHAT DID DI DO WHEN THE LIGHTS WENT OUT?'), and a photograph and caption of Prince William. He and his brother had spent the previous day visiting a police station ('YOUNG WILL JOINS THE OLD BILL!').

'We've no axe to grind'

Of course the tabloid Press aims to provide entertainment as well as news, and their choice of lead stories sometimes reflects this. But many of the decisions made by the news media reflect a particular point of view.

Most newspapers would claim to be presenting the facts without distortion. In TV, both BBC and ITN have a legal obligation to be accurate and impartial in their news coverage. But 'bias' in the news is not just a regrettable tendency.

It is something which is unavoidable if news is to be reported at all.

But the result is that the illusion that we are being told 'what really happened' is misleading. 'Eyewitness accounts' are not so authoritative as they seem. A photograph which seems to verify the story may not do so at all.

> **Bias is unavoidable if news is to be reported at all.**

While we are receiving the news, we are being directed in a multitude of ways as to how to interpret it.

Let's look at some of the ways this happens.

'Now, Mr Jones, are you really trying to tell me . . .?'

An interview seems to give you very nearly the whole truth. Somebody has been invited to give an account of events, aided by a professional whose job is to help that person communicate.

On TV we see the person actually speaking. In newspapers we are given his words transcribed.

Here is the story straight from the horse's mouth!

Or is it?

In reality, we hardly ever receive an unbiased version of events. Often what we see is decided by the editor.

For example, the broadcasting news media tend to accept the accounts of 'authoritative sources' (such as a government minister or a professor) as trustworthy. Few attempts are made to question their versions of events. An eyewitness of a demonstration will be allowed to speak unhindered.

Other sources (pressure group, political activist, trade union, *etc.*) are often treated as much less reliable. They are often challenged. ('Is that *really* what happened?') Statements of belief are questioned. Individuals are put on trial. Much of the interview time is spent in questioning credibility.

There are several reasons for this. Some are understandable and proper. But such techniques can interfere with the process of saying 'what actually happened'. If a large part of the evidence is never looked at, facts may be distorted or left out altogether.

It looks pretty violent from where I'm standing

In the historic miners' strike of 1984-5, the news photographs consistently showed the police defending themselves against angry pickets.

There was a reason for this. The camera crews were bringing expensive microphones and other equipment into an angry and potentially explosive situation. The safest place to photograph from was behind police lines.

So you never saw any shots by which to assess the miners' claim that there was police aggression. You saws incidents of miners' aggression. Because of the camera angle, you saw them threatening *you*. And when you saw the police, they were always on the defensive.

I'm not suggesting that the miners were necessarily justified in their accusations against the police. As a TV viewer rather than an eyewitness, I have no visual basis for deciding that. The placing of the cameras, necessary though it may have been, prevented any of us from reaching a true opinion from the camera evidence we had.

I always photograph best from the left

Mrs Thatcher listened to a conference debate for three hours, her face attentive and thoughtful — a 'public' face. But a photographer caught her off-guard, yawning. The anti-Tory newspaper gratefully seized on the photo and used it to accompany a report of the conference.

Mr Kinnock, newly elected Labour Party leader, went on a sea-shore walk with his wife for the benefit of Press photographers. He fell into the water. Hundreds of photographs of the Labour leader were taken that day; serious, statesmanlike photos expressing personality and purpose. The Tory newspapers used the one of him falling over.

News pictures affect how we respond to news. A good photo editor or film researcher will usually have several to choose from, and will make the choice with great care.

Different photographers recording the same event produce very different photographs. Timing, camera angle, lighting and other factors all play their part. You can capture somebody in a photograph that is quite uncharacteristic of him or her.

Which, in reporting, may have its uses.

A good example was the reporting of Mrs Victoria Gillick's campaign to compel doctors to consult parents, before prescribing contraceptives for children.

Mrs Gillick has striking looks. She has dark eyes and a mobile, expressive mouth. Newspapers favourable to her cause used

With appropriately edited transcripts, images can powerfully reinforce a particular interpretation.

photographs which made the most of her features.

Newspapers opposed to her cause, however, tended to use photographs in which her eyes looked staring, and her mouth was either thinly disapproving or vehemently declaiming.

Used with appropriately edited transcripts of her remarks, both images could powerfully reinforce a particular interpretation of Mrs Gillick's case.

Giving the truth a helping hand

Sometimes the newspapers and broadcast media simply tell untruths.

On the simplest level, some newspapers are

known to create stories where none exist. In my work as a writer I have worked with people who deny comments attributed to them in the media. From reliable information I know that it was physically impossible for the interviews ever to have taken place as claimed.

It's distressing that newspapers should tell lies. It's important we should know they do, because often a latent awe of the media makes us tend to reject the possibility. But it happens relatively rarely, usually (when cases come to court) in tabloid journalism.

More significant, and more justifiable, is the kind of fabrication where a photo that seems to record a single event is actually a composite of several photos. The reader is hardly ever aware that this has been done.

For example, one newspaper wanting to portray the variety of people queueing to sign the memorial book for Eisenhower at the American Embassy combined several photographs of the queue taken at different times.

Often such an image tells us more about an event than a simple photograph could. Sometimes it is the only way of capturing the essential truth of a situation. It is like a cartoon. In one sense a cartoon isn't true (Prince Charles's ears aren't *really* that big . . .) but it achieves an instantly recognizable likeness.

Somewhere between these two extremes is a third kind of falsification. The news media have sometimes so distorted facts that what is finally printed amounts to a deliberate lie.

An example of this is the wonderful but probably untrue story of the bishop who was met on his arrival in New York by a journalist.

'Do you plan to visit any nightclubs in New York?' demanded the journalist provocatively.

'*Are* there any nightclubs in New York?' was the puzzled response.

The headline next day read: 'BISHOP'S FIRST QUESTION: ARE THERE ANY NIGHTCLUBS IN NEW YORK?'

> **Like advertising, sub-headings influence most strongly when they are least noticed.**

This is a sub-heading

A final example of how we are directed to respond to news, even as we are receiving it, comes from newspapers.

In order to make reading easier, newspapers insert sub-headings between sections of a story. Usually they are a word or words taken from the main text and printed larger.

Sub-headings can be much more than emphasis. By emphasizing one word out of a whole quotation or description, they can direct our response to a story. They can control how we read it.

We are being influenced as well as informed,

Here is the news?

Here are three accounts of an incident in the miners' strike of 1984-5, published on the same day in three national daily newspapers.

In each case, what appears to be factual reporting is actually slanted; you are being directed, as you read, *how* to read. For example:

● Discrepancy: Were 70 or 101 people held?
● Loaded sub-heads: the *Sun* clearly blames the miners — 'demo mob', 'vicious', 'hurt', 'rampage' all create a picture of uncontrollable rioting.
   The *Telegraph's* language is much cooler — 'clash' is a neutral word — but the sub-heading conveys police control: 'Police horses go in'.
● Pictures: the *Sun's* picture is heavily anti-miner.

Who has the correct version? Probably none of them. You will get nearer the truth the more accounts you read, and the closer you look at the 'small print'.

70 held in pit demo clashes

Violence after London rally

By ALAN LAW

MOUNTED policemen and officers in riot gear were sent in to disperse demonstrators in Whitehall yesterday after a rally to support the miners.

Demonstrators accused the police of violence as two walls of officers pushed them along Whitehall to clear it.

As running fights broke out one officer pushed a man to the ground and, according to demonstrators, kicked him several times. Bystanders clashed with police as they dragged the man to safety.

Seconds later, six policemen picked up another man and threw him towards the crowd.

Arrests

Earlier several officers had been hurt in clashes in Whitehall.

In all, there were more than 70 arrests. But at least two were freed when demonstrators staged a sit-down to protest.

Thirty thousand people attended a rally in Trafalgar Square after a march from Hyde Park.

Miners' leader Arthur Scargill told the strikers and their supporters at the rally: "We will not be beaten into submission."

He urged them to stand firm to "save our integrity and jobs," and he attacked other trade unions for not giving the NUM full support.

Mr. Scargill said he would meet the TUC's "inner cabinet" today, and he would make fresh approaches to its General Secretary, Norman Willis.

His speech was frequently interrupted by loud applause, and at the end he was given an ovation.

Other speakers at the rally included Labour MP Tony Benn.

Mirror

and this is so whether we're reading the *Star* or the *Financial Times*. And the sub-heads are effectively invisible. Like advertising, they influence most strongly when they are least noticed.

For these and many other reasons, it may appear that one of the major untruths of the media is their claim to tell the truth.

The question of truth

'This is Mrs X,' we are told. 'Mrs X was X's first wife. She knows him. She is prepared to tell you about him. She will give you the facts.' (She usually has quite an axe to grind as well,

101 HELD IN WHITEHALL PIT CLASH
NCB seek record return today

MOUNTED police were brought in to disperse a Central London demonstration in support of the miners yesterday—the eve of what the Coal Board hopes will be a record return to work at collieries.

Whitehall was sealed as the rally went on in Trafalgar Square and in ugly scenes of violence 101 people were arrested.

The leader of the Yorkshire miners, Mr Jack Taylor, admitted in a television interview that the strike would end with a drift back, but that a "type of guerrilla warfare" would ensue. Mr Arthur Scargill, at the Trafalgar Square rally, compared the strike to a "second world war resistance movement."

After the vote the 29,000 working Nottinghamshire miners to call off the national 15-month overtime ban, the Energy Secretary, Mr Walker, predicted that coal stocks at power stations would begin to rise next month.

Other pit news—P1; Pictures—Back Page;
Editorial Comment—P18

Police horses go in
By ALAN COPPS

ONE hundred and one people were arrested, and several including a number of police, were injured when a London demonstration in support of the striking miners broke up in ugly scenes of violence yesterday.

Police initially blamed "a hooligan element"—clearly not miners — for scuffles which broke out at the end of Whitehall just as Mr Scargill was addressing the rally in Trafalgar Square.

The result of those minor clashes Whitehall was sealed off by lines of police and the later more serious violence broke out in a section of the crowd frustrated that it had never reached the Square.

Placard shafts hurled at police

Eventually 20 police horses were called in to disperse part of the crowd which had jammed across Whitehall just beside Horse Guards Parade.

In scenes reminiscent of the picket lines which many of the marchers had left, the crowd eventually broke into small groups.

As the horses moved in three-deep lines of police on foot cleared the length of Whitehall between the confrontation and Trafalgar Square, where by then the rally was breaking up peacefully.

Several groups were driven by police down side routes towards the Embankment, where a fleet of coaches which had brought hundreds of marchers from out of town was parked.

During the clashes a police motorcycle was turned on its side in Northumberland Avenue, and missiles, including the shafts from placards and empty drink cans, were hurled at police. Apart from the use of the horses there was no sign of riot gear.

Red and black anarchist flags were prominent among the banners of those most closely involved in the violence. Four policemen needed hospital treatment and one with a head injury was detained overnight as a precaution.

Mr Scargill apparently un-

aware of the clashes as he spoke, said the strike had begun a "resistance movement similar to the one that worked throughout the Second World War."

It was "the most historic strike in the history of this or possibly any other" country," he said.

It was a result of this dispute. The issue that brought the miners out was the policy to close pits. There is no way that this trade union is going to put our signatures to an agreement to close pits and axe jobs."

He spoke of the suffering of mining communities and paid tribute to the "8,500 miners injured and the four people who have died on picket lines." The fight to save our jobs is even more important than it was a year ago.

'Dishonourable men' on TUC

Later, asked about the weekend remarks by Mr Walker, Energy Secretary, branding him as "foolish, pathetic and stupid," Mr Scargill said: "Mr Walker has made this dispute more personal than he has in the past.

"I think it shows an act of desperation on their part. I will deal only with the issues and let him be judged by others."

Other speakers both before the march and at the rally include Mr Wedgwood Benn, Labour MP for Chesterfield, Mr Kenneth Livingstone, leader of the Greater London Council, and Mr Mick McGahey, miners' vice-president, who made a bitter attack on the lack of TUC support for the strikers.

Mr McGahey said there were three types of union leader on the General Council of the TUC: "Honourable men" like the leaders of the seamen's, railways and print unions who had fought for

Continued on Back P, Col 5

101 HELD AS PIT DEMO MOB GO ON RAMPAGE
Nine hurt in scuffles

MORE than 100 people were arrested yesterday as pit strike violence erupted in the heart of London.

Pitched battles broke out in Whitehall as more than 15,000 chanting demonstrators marched to a rally in Trafalgar Square.

Nine people were taken to hospital.

By ANNETTE WITHERIDGE

They were four policemen including a P.C. who was detained overnight, and five civilians.

Several other officers had cuts and bruises.

There were 101 arrests.

Police blamed a group of about 200 drunken hotheads for the skirmishes.

Cheering

Fists and boots flew as beer cans were lobbed through the air.

Police reinforcements arrived from both ends of Whitehall, squeezing the demonstrators into a brawling mass outside Horseguards Parade.

Wooden staves from various banners were hurled at officers.

Miners and their families were joined on the march by peace campaigners—and a banner-waving group from Lesbians Against Pit Closures.

I saw men and women dragged screaming and fighting from the battleground.

I could see frightened children crying as their parents held them in the air for safety, and I saw cups of scalding coffee hurled at the police.

Vicious

Mr Scargill was unaware of the trouble as he addressed the rally a few hundred yards away in Trafalgar Square.

He said the strike had begun a "resistance movement similar to the one which worked throughout the Second World War."

Scottish miners' president Mick McGahey told the cheering crowd.

fight goes on. We've come too far to turn back."

And Left-winger Tony Benn claimed it was a massive demonstration of support for the dispute.

He said: "This is the biggest demonstration to be held in London for many years—perhaps the biggest there has ever been."

Kevin Halpin, the rally's chief organiser, accused police of breaking an agreement to allow stewards to deal with minor incidents.

Hurt

And he added: "This Government has shown its most vicious in living memory. We have learned of the repressive powers of the State, sending in police to beat down striking miners."

He accused one legal system and the Government of declaring war on the miners.

Demonstrator tangles with a police inspector Picture by BRENDAN BEIRNE

Sun

Telegraph

59

but this is not mentioned!)

'Cheque-book journalism', in which newspapers trade on people's vulnerability and financial need (and sometimes their desire for fleeting fame), relies on finding individuals close to the story. It adds the lustre of authenticity to what is already sensation.

The fact that usually no attempt is made to check the story or to hear alternative viewpoints doesn't change matters.

Even the trashiest tabloid newspaper will advertise its latest exposé of the sex escapades of a rock musician or film star by claiming to give you the truth.

But the claim is made throughout the Press. 'Quality' papers compete with each other by claiming authority and comprehensiveness. They claim to be reflecting accurately the concerns and priorities of the public.

What is the truth?

Underlying the whole matter is the question of what truth is anyway.

If by 'truth' we mean an accurate, totally unbiased, comprehensive and objectively presented version of events, then we will never find perfection in the media.

In many cases there is not the will to provide it; in all cases there is no hope of providing it. Space demands that news be edited. But as soon as decisions are made to edit out some aspects in preference to others, interpretation has started.

So should we abandon the quest for truth in the media?

By no means.

God is truth

When, as Jesus Christ, God walked upon the earth, he called himself the Truth (*John 14:6*). Nothing is more important than truth for a Christian. It's who God is. 'Let God be true, and every man a liar,' says Paul (*Romans 3:4*).

Physical limitations don't bother him. When he looks at history and what mankind is doing,

> **It appears that one of the major untruths of the media is their claim to tell the truth.**

he doesn't have to depend on a selection of the evidence. His mind isn't limited. No human being could know, let alone assess, every fact in a situation. But God does.

He is *fair*. He isn't prejudiced or biased. He doesn't have favourites (*Acts 10:34*). He hates cheating of any kind (*e.g. Amos 8:4-6*).

There are eleven words used for 'truth' in the Bible. One — the Hebrew *emeth* — is often used about God. It means 'steadfastness'. The media, however much or little they try, can never reveal truth in its fullness. But God is dependable, steadfast and true.

And because he is true, what he says is true. 'All your commands are *true*,' declares the psalmist (*Psalm 119:151*). If we follow God, we are following the truth.

Getting near the truth

This means that the closer that human interpretations approach the perspective and truth of God — whether or not it's Christians who are doing the interpreting — the more we can meaningfully call them 'true'.

It means that even though an interview cannot avoid distorting the facts to some extent, it need not twist the truth out of all recognition.

If the interviewer knows that an interview can distort, and compensates by ensuring that the person interviewed is given a fair chance to express his views as clearly as possible, the interview will reflect something of real justice and truth.

There is a place, of course, for probing interviews and investigative journalism.

But reporting and journalism which are concerned for truth will work on the basis that everybody has *some* sort of axe to grind.

Being a government minister doesn't automatically mean you're going to be completely balanced and fair. Being a trade-union spokesperson doesn't mean you have to be cross-examined twice as hard as a surgeon or a policeman.

> **No human being could know, let alone assess, every fact in a situation. But God does.**

Media in search of truth will seek to verify *all* versions of events, not simply those given by 'suspect' sources.

And all the devices and techniques we've been considering in this chapter will be used in an attempt to reveal the truth, not deliberately to mislead the audience.

This kind of search for truth isn't restricted to people who claim to be Christians. We are all made in the image of God. Broadcasters and journalists who are not Christians can want the truth. And many of them do.

Was that quite fair?
A checklist for interviews

- Did the interviewer introduce the interview in such a way that you were already forming an opinion before the interview started?
- Was the person who was interviewed given a fair chance to explain him/herself?
- Did it seem that the interviewer approached the interview with previously set ideas about what he/she expected to find out?
- Was the person interviewed allowed to complete sentences?
- Was the tone of the interview relaxed/ hostile/complimentary?
- Do you think the person interviewed left the studio feeling reasonably fairly dealt with?
- Did the interviewer say anything to the audience after the person being interviewed had left? Do you think it affected your view of what had been said?

Give me a place to stand

Yet the news media still contain conflicting interests, contradictory versions, material inaccuracies and vested interests.

Sometimes it seems that we can never get at the truth. The mass of fleeting information, presented to us day by day, can appear like a shifting quicksand, sucking in data and processing it before it has a chance to assume identifiable shape.

We need a place to stand back from it all. We need an absolute standard, with which to evaluate the changing patterns of the modern world.

The Bible tells us that in God, we have such a reference point, by which — by whom — we can look at our world and its activities.

Ways of testing the news

The most important thing when we receive news is, not to regard it as infallible or unquestionable truth.

1. Have you heard the same story from another news source? Are there any discrepancies?
2. Who is providing eye-witness reports/ comment? Are these people entirely objective? If eye-witnesses, were they in a good position to see what really happened?
3. Where were the cameras located?
4. Is the incident part of a wider story, and how helpful is it to take it out of context?
5. Is our understanding of the incident being affected by the items that have preceded and followed it in the news?
6. Does the organization/agency/newspaper/ programme reporting this item stand to benefit in any way by a less than objective presentation?
7. Are you left with the feeling that a reasonable selection of facts has been put in front of you from which you can form a valid opinion of the item?

chapter five

The media as preachers

In George Orwell's frightening vision of *Nineteen Eighty-Four,* the people gather in public places dominated by huge screens. The face of the Leader is everywhere. Hugely magnified, Big Brother's features confront the population as he exhorts and encourages them.

In every private home, telescreens which cannot be turned off pour out propaganda. The Ministry of Truth — 'which concerned itself with news, entertainment, education and the fine arts' — towers over London, proclaiming and eavesdropping at the same time.

In the world beyond London, Eurasia is at war with Oceania. In the libraries, government agents are cutting history books to pieces and destroying files and documents. History is being made, and unmade.

It is a picture of a society whose leaders are totally in command of the mass media.

> **"**
> **We should carry on constant propaganda among the people on the facts of world progress and the bright future ahead, so that they will build their confidence in victory.**
> **"**

Mao Tse-Tung, *Quotations* ('The Thoughts of Chairman Mao'), Peking, 1966, p. 70.

When the real 1984 arrived, it seemed at first glance that Orwell had got it wrong. Government was not concentrated into four giant ministries. A global war was not raging between two superpowers. Private homes did not have compulsory indoctrination screens.

But Orwell's fantasy was not a vision of the future at all. '1984' is simply the numbers '1948' switched around. He was writing about his own times.

In 1948, he realized that control of the media

is an indispensable weapon in securing control of the minds and hearts of the people. History since has proved him right.

Every successful revolutionary has understood the power of the media.

In China, the wall-poster has been a crucially important tool of social change. The printed word has had a major role in a newly literate mass population. The *Thoughts of Chairman Mao,* printed and distributed to millions, kept the revolution going and continually refreshed it.

In the Soviet Union, the official news agency, Tass, is monitored by Western observers. They have often noted the complete omission of news of certain events happening outside the Soviet Union. For the Soviet people, modern history has in effect been rewritten.

(At the same time, it would be naive not to accept that all governments censor news. It may be to protect national security; British governments have restricted news coverage of every recent war on these grounds. It may be for political advantage; most governments will try to distract the public from unfavourable trade or employment figures. But it happens. Usually, it ought not to.)

In the West, advertising has often brought about social change.

Sometimes the change has been political. For example, there have been some well-known advertising campaigns associated with British general elections. At least one advertising consultancy — Saatchi and Saatchi — has become famous for its part in an electoral victory.

Other changes have been more gradual, though just as significant.

For example, the media sustained a massive youth market in the 1960s. Clothes, records, and entertainment made vast fortunes for individuals and generated healthy foreign exchange for the government.

The sixties revolution was a revolution of ideas. It was also a revolution of style. But

> **Without the media the sixties would not have seen a revolution at all.**

without the media, it would not have been a revolution at all.

Come back George, all is forgiven

Prophecy or not, Orwell's portrait of the year '1984' was remarkably close to the truth — with one major difference. The media today are not so visible and not so forceful as in his novel.

TV sets *are* in almost every home in the country, but they are there by choice rather than compulsion — Orwell would probably have been amused to find that we actually pay for them ourselves.

We do not attend the media at compulsory times in order to be indoctrinated, as in Orwell's vision.

And we are not secretly watched by the media for every hour of our waking day.

But lower visibility does not impair the media's power to influence. The soap-box is smaller, but the media are still preaching. Orwell was right. As we shall see.

Pulpit mannerisms

In any media communication, what seems to be the main statement is often less significant than what is communicated by other, non-verbal elements. More is said than what is spoken, and, like an onion, meaning in the media has many layers.

What I have called preaching is sometimes called 'media rhetoric'. Often it just means that statements are never made in isolation. Colours, clothes, how you point the camera, the sort of questions you ask, and many other factors all have something to say as well. We have already seen how this works.

But often the media use these hidden levels of meaning to communicate much more powerfully than they could with words alone.

This is preaching: it attempts to change our minds; and it tries to do so in two ways.

I'm gonna tell you how it's gonna be

As I write, the main political news story is the

> **Often the media use hidden levels of meaning to communicate much more powerfully than with words alone.**

proposed merger between the Liberal and SDP parties. The *Daily Mail's* sympathies have been with Dr David Owen of the SDP, who is against the present merger.

In reporting the story, the *Mail* has not attempted to hide its views. 'STEEL: OWEN WAS TO BLAME,' said a front-page headline in September 1987. In case readers were in danger of missing the point, the story continued: 'In a brazen display of political buck passing, Mr Steel accused Dr Owen of being "the real culprit"' (for the parties' failure in the 1987 General Election). A later headline said simply 'STEEL MUST GO'.

This is the media used as explicit propaganda. It is saying, 'I will tell you how things *ought* to be.' Nobody who reads the *Daily Mail* is in danger of thinking that it is not a Conservative newspaper. The editorial viewpoint is clear to see.

Newspapers have traditionally used their editorials, leader or main articles and front pages to argue for change. They are useful voice in a free society. Sometimes they have campaigned for necessary social change and reform.

Because they are so visible, media statements like these raise few practical problems for a Christian. When you know what is being said, you can decide whether or not you agree with it.

Life's like that really, isn't it ...?

If the media only preached like that — by shouting a message and backing it up with all the techniques and skills available to them — they wouldn't be much more than enormous soap boxes.

But the real power of the media lies in the fact that they don't just represent. They *create*.

The media decide what events constitute 'news'. For 'serious' programmes, like *Newsnight* and *Panorama,* somebody decides what topics will be discussed. They decide whether sex or skiing will have most space in the next issue of

Think positive

The power of the media is like that of the tongue. Both are agents of communication; both can do great good or great harm. James says that the effects of the tongue are like those of a forest fire (*James 3:3-12*). He goes on to say that we can choose with the same tongue to praise God or curse people.

The power which the media generally use to reflect a non-Christian view can also be harnessed as a powerful tool to proclaim the gospel.

For example, Paul's sufferings and his message were big news (*Philippians 1:12-13*). People who wanted the latest news about this extraordinary prisoner couldn't help picking up something of the gospel.

● What are some of the ways that the media could be used by Christians?
● Do you know any ways Christians are using them today?
● How effective do you think using the media in this way is?

a magazine. Media planning even decides at what time of day or night we will watch a particular programme.

It's not just 'serious' programmes that are preselected in this way. The decision that what the British public needs is yet another Australian soap opera, a magazine serial about a Victorian governess, six weeks of darts and/or snooker coverage — is out of our hands.

The public has very little say. We are a majority interest with few voting rights.

Of course this is inevitable to some extent, and it would be impossible for the media programme and editorial planners to operate as a consultative body.

But it emphasizes that the media create what we see, and read, and accept as normal. When we look at the media we are not looking at a reflection of life as it is. We are looking at something which has been put together by media people.

A star among stars

Russell Grant is an astrologer. He has become a media celebrity. He regularly appears on television and in the Press, giving horoscope predictions and talking about star-signs.

He became famous on breakfast television, giving horoscope readings and counselling viewers on how they should prepare for the day ahead.

He was longer on air than *Thought for the Day,* and was warmly supported by the other presenters, who plied him with interested questions.

No Christian spokesman has had such an opportunity to present his or her beliefs on horoscopes to the viewers.

Do you think they should? Is television being fair?

Missing the mark

Most of the time the media view of the world is close enough to reality to cause few problems.

But sometimes, the media create a picture of reality which is far from true. Then by repeating it over and over again, they make it *seem* to be true.

The kind of 'preaching' we have just been looking at says, 'This is how things *ought* to be.'

Now we are talking about media preaching that says, 'This is how things *really are;* believe me.' But it's an untruth.

A wide range of ideologies are presented to us in this way. Let's look at three examples.

The way it is

In *EastEnders,* people from outside the East End are treated with suspicion. A different voice is a liability. So are different hobbies. Cultured interests can also set a character apart.

Debbie Wilkins, who had a middle-class voice, didn't fit into the narrow class structure of Albert Square. James Willmott-Brown, the publican, spoke and lived quite differently from the rest of the cast. He became a symbol of the yuppie invasion of the East End. In storylines he was set against the East End community.

There's a repeated emphasis on the traditions of the East End. Lou Beale, Ethel Skinner and Dr Legg represent the older generation, and often reminisce about the old days.

The picture that is presented is that of a self-sufficient community, defined by class. Twice a week, we're shown that this is what true community is; caring, compassionate, and able to look after its own.

It's an illusory picture.

For example, as in most soaps, Christianity doesn't figure large in *EastEnders*. Dot Cotton claims to be a Christian, but rarely says anything which has a cutting edge. Most of the time, Dot's Christianity is part of her dithering, comic, helpless character.

And, says *EastEnders,* that is as much Christianity as anyone needs; for here is a whole community of people getting on with life, supporting each other, laughing with each other, crying with each other. Who needs God?

But British society doesn't operate that way. Eleven per cent of us have a meaningful Christian commitment; many more have nominal links with Christianity; and Christian churches and projects play a significant part in the life of the inner cities.

Meanwhile, *EastEnders* gets on with the running of its own universe.

> **If TV were utterly realistic, true Christian values would occasionally be aired without compromise. If TV were depicting life as it really is, the place of faith in the lives of believers would be recognized and shown for what it is, just as in real life.**
>
> Stephen R. Lawhead, *Turn Back the Night,* Crossway, 1985, p. 57.

Spreading the word in Street, Square and Close

How would you introduce a biblically Christian character into one of the popular soap operas? Would it be possible? What sort of storylines would you develop, and how would you link them in to existing ones?

The ladies, God bless 'em

The media have a bias against women.

At the most obvious level, women are simply kept out of things. So we get used to the fact that not many women (compared to men) appear on TV. And because it's how things are, we tend to accept it.

We accept that not many women reach senior posts on newspapers. We become used to the fact that women are supposed to do 'women's work' (writing a woman's page in a newspaper, or reading the news — and that was a major breakthrough — or presenting a fashion programme).

But the discrimination exists at other levels. Stereotypes of the housewife and the breadwinning male persist long after a significant number of British households have the husband unemployed. Women in adverts are often presented as possessions.

Women's bodies are used to sell everything from insurance to computer stationery.

It is a false view of the value of women. But because it is so often restated by the media, it perpetuates itself.

Christians should be deeply concerned about this. Sexual stereotypes have no part in biblical Christianity. Yet each day we are exposed to them, and invited to accept them as normal.

They're even bringing religion into Christmas now

A major problem for Christians is the anti-Christian ideology that pervades the media.

It is presented by simply ignoring the religious dimension of life.

Adverts promote their products as essential for a perfect, relaxed Sunday — but church has no part in it.

Agony columns in newspapers feature letters from people who appear to have real spiritual problems. Yet the replies give no hint that an answer might be found by consulting a

> **Stereotypes of the housewife and the breadwinning male persist long after a significant number of British households have the husbands unemployed.**

". . .and four out of five men wouldn't change. . ."

clergyman, or by prayer, or by anything religious at all.

The underlying assumption is that God is irrelevant. He is not needed.

In *Dallas,* which is set in America's Bible belt, church is portrayed as irrelevant.

Christians have two reasons to be concerned about this.

● First: millions of people are receiving, from the media, the impression that God has nothing relevant to say about modern life.

● Second: the media have the power to question our faith and even to damage it. If we aren't careful, we could end up as broken Christians. And the media are so pervasive, and their influence is often so subtle, that we might never find out why.

Biblical principles

The Bible has a great deal to say about our vulnerability to influence, and the dangers of incomplete portrays of reality.

Luke describes a riot in Ephesus in which most of the rioters had no idea why they were there (*Acts 19: 29-34*). They had been influenced. And the influence had been at a deep, subconscious level.

The danger of half-truth or incomplete truth represented as reality appears very early in the Bible.

In *Genesis 3,* the serpent brilliantly persuades Eve to accept a version of reality which is not true. By making up a half-true story and then repeating it persuasively, he makes it seem that what he says is the truth (*Genesis 3:1-5*).

> **Throughout the Bible, the partly true and the incompletely true are shown to be enemies of truth.**

Throughout the Bible, the partly true and the incompletely true are shown to be the enemies of truth.

'We decided to give *all* the proceeds to the church,' said Ananias and Sapphira (*Acts 5:1-11*). It wasn't a very big untruth — they kept only part of the money for themselves. But the lie killed them.

'I'm sure Naaman would want me to have

some reward too,' said Gehazi, and asked for the gift Elisha had turned down (*2 Kings 5:15-27*). Naaman could easily afford it; but Gehazi and his descendants were cursed with leprosy because of the untruth.

How to judge the media's messages

Here are three tests which may help:

- Is the advert, film, programme, *etc. well made?* Is the article well written? Is the craftsmanship good?

  If the person who made it can't be bothered to do a competent job, why should you spend any more time on it? There is lots of sloppy work around in the media. Don't encourage it. Don't buy it.

- Has the work got *integrity?* Do you feel that the person who made it has some belief in it? Or is is a 'positive message' couched in unspoken cynicism and shallow commercialism?

  If it doesn't have any ring of truth at all, give it a miss. If the author doesn't believe in it, why should you?

- Is the message *true?* If a person is singing about relationships, for example, what is being commended? Loving people, or using them? If it's a newspaper article about a national tragedy, is there a genuine sense of grieving — or a routine shock-horror treatment?

If you're a Christian you will probably find quite a lot to challenge you in media presentations that score two out of three above. Anything that scores three out of three will be something well worth spending time on, enjoying, and learning from.

Putting it into practice

What then should a Christian's response be?

Take stock

It's a good idea occasionally to do a media stock-take. What newspaper do you read most often? What TV programmes do you watch? What adverts are you most often exposed to?

List them, and then try to identify what, in each case, is the underlying message. Where are the media coming from? What view of reality are they expressing? What do they say about men and women? About God? About how to deal with the human problems of loneliness, poverty, and so on?

Take heed

When you have done this you may decide that living biblically means that you must make some changes. You may want to take a different newspaper, watch a different programme, have a different approach to adverts.

You may, on the other hand, decide not to make any changes.

Whichever of the two it may be, it's *essential* for our spiritual growth and Christian discipleship that we cultivate a critical eye for the media. We should always be aware that facts are not neutral. There is always an underlying message.

Take heart

You may feel rather overwhelmed by the sheer power of the media. How can we possibly cope? How can we protect ourselves against being influenced, often without our knowledge and against our will?

We have grounds for confidence. The Holy Spirit, as we read the Bible, will guide us into 'all truth' (*John 16:13*). And being guided into truth, we will be able more and more to discern what is really true, and reject what is false.

When Jesus prayed for us as we go into the world, he asked that we should be sanctified by

> **Facts are not neutral: there is always an underlying message.**

the truth. And he continued: 'Your word is truth' (*John 17:17*).

God's truth is not *just* a perfect standard against which we can measure rival ideologies, though it is certainly that.

The truth has the power to sanctify us — to *change our lives*. We don't have to change them by ourselves.

Christian salestalk

The world is presenting us with all sorts of messages and propaganda for various causes.

Should Christians strike back?

Is there a place for

- Christian books?
- Christian films (especially ones released in major cinemas, like some of the Billy Graham films)?
- Christian advertising?
- Christian music?

Are the techniques of modern media advertising appropriate for evangelism? If not, why not?

If Christianity is our 'product', what should be our market? Is it right to use terms like these about evangelism?

chapter six

Living with the media

We began this book by looking at the media as a whole, and the debate that surrounds them. Then we looked at four different aspects of the media in turn. In each we were able to identify areas for concern, and to begin to apply a biblical perspective to the media.

The subject of the media is a fascinating one which could have filled a much larger book. Indeed, the literature of media studies is large and growing.

But this is an issue which is more than an intriguing debating topic. The media touch and influence the lives of all of us. If we allow them to, they will mould our thinking and form our opinions for us.

We will, in Paul's words, be letting the world around us squeeze us into its own mould (*Romans 12:2*).

And so we must have a plan of action.

Dumping Dallas – the option of rejection

Some Christians have dealt with the problem of the media by throwing them out of their lives completely.

They have no television in their homes. They use the radio sparingly. They don't buy newspapers or magazines (except Christian ones). They ignore advertising. In fact because of their general approach to the media they see relatively little advertising anyway.

I don't want to suggest that such choices are wrong for every Christian. For some families and individuals it will be a right and necessary course of action. But for the majority of us, I think it would be a mistake. There are several reasons.

Cornflakes with Wogan

The first and simplest reason is that it would be virtually impossible anyway. Even if we removed the obvious media — the newspapers, the television — we would still be exposed to media influences.

The packet of cornflakes on our breakfast table was probably bought because advertising influenced us towards that brand. We may well not have realized we were looking at advertisements — familiarity had probably made them invisible to us. But they worked.

Similarly, we might not buy newspapers, but we almost certainly see other people's. And even if we have no television, we are probably familiar with a wide variety of personalities and programmes which have become well-known far beyond the screen. Thousands of people who do not have a television know who Terry Wogan is.

Sex, violence and worldliness

In the Christian community, the media have often been mistrusted. This attitude has often been linked with the problem of 'worldliness'.

From this viewpoint television and newspapers are to be dealt with very cautiously, because both contain large amounts of explicit violence and explicit sex. They display scepticism which often becomes blasphemy.

So Christians holding the 'rejection' view of the media will often point to verses such as *Philippians 4:8* ('. . . if anything is excellent or praiseworthy — think about such things').

'After all,' they may well point out, 'the media bring the world into your home. And we know that the world is evil. It's a dangerous influence on Christians.'

But Paul in Philippians makes *truth* a priority. 'Whatever is true, whatever is noble, whatever is right . . .'. We should be thinking about things

> **From this viewpoint, television and newspapers are to be dealt with very cautiously. . . . containing large amounts of explicit violence and sex . . . displaying scepticism which often becomes blasphemy.**

79

that are true, not just things that make us feel good.

And we've seen throughout this book that though truth in the media is a complex matter, it is not a lost cause. We live in a fallen world, and for most of us the media are an essential part of our finding our way around it.

Jesus sent us *into* the world (*Matthew 28:19*). He knew what sort of a world it was, but he specifically did not want Christians to be pulled out of it. He prayed for us like this: 'My prayer is not that you take them out of the world but that you protect them from the evil one' (*John 17:15*).

If we want to communicate the gospel, we should be particularly interested in the media; but there is a risk.

Broadcasting the good news

A third reason why we should not reject the media is that through the media we can understand other people better.

If we want to communicate the gospel, we should be particularly interested in the media.

There is a risk involved. Some Christians have become involved with the media and their faith has been damaged as a result. The support of your church and praying friends can be crucial. For some Christians it would be quite wrong to make a career in the media or become involved in some other way.

But some of us must, if we are to go out into the world and tell people about Jesus.

And all of us should learn to look at the media critically and with understanding. It's no use responding to interests and needs which don't exist. The media reflect the daily life of millions, and they are successful because they understand their audience.

Of course we should never reduce the sharing of the good news of Jesus to a mere technique or a cold strategy. But we can learn a lot from the media.

'To the Jews I became like a Jew . . . To those under the law I became like one under the law . . . To those not having the law I became like one not having the law . . . To the weak I became weak,' said Paul (*1 Corinthians 9:20-22*). Paul was always willing to sit where people sat, to listen to what was being said in the world at large.

He knew that the gospel is big enough to answer any question or need of mankind. So he made it his business to find out what those questions and needs were, and to make use of the first-century equivalent of the media (*e.g. Acts 17:17 ff.; 19:8-10*).

Bob Geldof, and other media plusses

Finally, one of the strongest reasons why the media shouldn't be thrown out of our lives is that there is much that is good about them.

The horrific extent of famine in Africa was brought to the attention of the world by the media.

The first information came in a documentary news report, using the full power of photography and the simple, stark images of dying children.

Then the pervasiveness and persuasiveness of the media were harnessed to mobilize and consolidate public concern. The use of film meant that we could almost be there, witnessing the tragedy in person.

Bob Geldof's role was made easier by the fact that he was a media person. He was already known as a rebel, somebody who had no time for convention and protocol.

And the ability of the media to speak to people directly, in every part of their daily lives, meant that projects like Band Aid were made known to many people who usually don't hear of relief projects.

It would be easy to list many other cases where the media have mobilized public concern and action.

The media don't merely maintain a presence in our society. They have a role.

In wartime, people look to the media for information and encouragement.

Churchill was as great a radio orator as a parliamentary one. In the Falklands War, Ian McDonald became a household name. It was his task to give the news briefings, and it was his solemn voice we heard announcing the latest developments.

In peacetime the media have a similar role. Local radio keeps people in touch, and by means of phone-ins can reach and often help directly the elderly and the sick. In the great hurricane of October 1987, local radio stations broadcast to stricken areas, telling them when they could expect their electricity, gas and water to be restored. They were a lifeline.

But even this is rather a utilitarian view of the media. Valuable though their role is, it's all too easy to accept the media *despite* themselves. We say that the end justifies the means, that the good things outweigh the bad.

But I think that as Christians we should also welcome the media for their own distinctive good qualities.

For example, television is at present the focus for a tremendous amount of creativity. There are excellent plays and documentaries. Some genuinely innovative work is being done.

Many of our best actors, actresses and writers are drawn to television.

More and more discussion programmes are appearing, of adequate length to grapple with important subjects. Television is beginning to be very good at this.

Excellence in the media is not a rare thing. It can be found in all of them. And they will enrich our lives.

And now for the bad news

As we have seen, however, the media do present problems. For Christians who have decided against rejecting the media, the problems resolve into two kinds.

Media stress

Many Christians who accept the presence of the media in their lives find that problems and strains can result just *because* the media are present.

They're perplexed, for example, about how best to handle television in the home. Should we make television a major part of our lives? Should we allow children to watch anything and everything? What about its effect on our domestic life, our church involvement, our relationships and our other activities?

There can even be problems with the news. How spiritually helpful is a daily diet of horror, disaster, and suffering?

It often seems that good news never gets into the newspapers. And the non-news material that helps to fill newspapers ranges from the trivial to soft-porn, with some newspapers hardly bothering with news at all.

There can be worries, too, about whether our witness will be affected if we are known to watch television, to take a particular newspaper, or be strongly influenced by advertising. Is it a case of leading one's 'weaker brethren' (and sisters) astray?

These are important questions, and can cause much heart-searching.

Some factors in media stress

- *EastEnders* 7.30—8pm (and Sunday omnibus); *Coronation Street* 7.30—8pm; *Neighbours* 5.30—6pm; *Brookside* 8—8.30pm (and Saturday omnibus): *etc.* Imagine a weekly diary with these times blocked in. Where are you going to squeeze in
  - your friends
  - college work
  - church activities
  - reading thinking praying, *etc.?*
- How many people have you seen killed this week in newspaper photos and TV news? What do you think the effect on you has been?
- Do you ever think life would be more manageable without a radio or television?
- What gets pushed out of your life so the media can be fitted in?

'Hands off, this is my happy hour'

A different type of problem is found by those Christians who accept the media into their lives so readily that they don't see any problems at all.

For them the media have become neutral territory. They go there for leisure, for entertainment — in some cases, for work.

The things they do on Sundays in church, their daily Bible reading and prayer-times, all have little to do with the media. Really they are irrelevant. Those things belong to a different compartment of their lives.

When they move from one to the other, Christianity can quite legitimately be left behind, to be picked up later.

Few of them would express it like that. But for most people who have this view of the media, double standards can easily and subtly take root.

Their tolerance level rises. They accept
- Bad language
- Gratuitous violence
- Contempt for women
- Racism
- Sick humour . . .

In church, or in the company of other Christians, they wouldn't accept such things. But when it's on television, or in the newspaper, or on a street hoarding, it's somehow different.

And sometimes they realize this, and it worries them.

A biblical response

So how do we resolve the problems, without sacrificing our Christian integrity?

Get to know your media

First, it's vital to come to terms with the media.

This book has, I hope, been a useful beginning. There are a number of resources which can take you further.

Most libraries and bookshops will have some books on the media. Try to find books which tackle how the media operate, and also ones which tackle the media as a cultural phenomenon.

On soap opera, have a look at some of the coffee-table books which are produced to give you the background to your favourite soap — they are often illuminating.

Read books by newspaper reporters and news photographers. Some Fleet Street editors have written about their work and what they see as being the role of the Press in today's world. At least one tabloid journalist has written his account of how he handled a major news story

(Harry Arnold of the *Sun*, in *Charles and Diana: a Royal Love Story*, New English Library, 1981).

Secondly, listen to the media themselves. Few voices in our culture are so self-conscious as the media. They often examine their origins, their methods and their reason for existence.

Francis Wheen's television series *Television* is available in book form (Century, 1985) and the series will no doubt be repeated. Newspaper leaders and editorials often give a good idea of what the newspaper thinks its role is. There are a number of similar resources offering the chance to hear what the media think they are all about.

More explicitly, the media have several self-policing Authorities, Complaints Commissions, and so on.

The Press Council, for example, exists to maintain standards in the Press and hears complaints from within and outside the profession. If judgment is made against a newspaper, the newspaper is under a moral obligation to publish the Council's findings in its own pages.

The Press Council

The Press Council, 1 Salisbury Square, London EC4Y 8AE

The Advertising Standards Authority, Brook House, Torrington Place, London WC1E 7HN.

The Advertising Standards Authority was established to promote 'legal, decent, honest and truthful' advertising. Complaints are investigated thoroughly, and where upheld the offending advertiser is given a strong warning. Recent ASA cases have taken a strong line on exploitation of women in advertising, for example.

Both bodies have few statutory powers, but are respected and their rulings are usually heeded. Their publications, which you can find in local libraries, are a useful resource.

Often, when one examines the guidelines

> **Share the experience with others ... see a programme with a group of friends ... discuss it afterwards.**

and standards proposed by the media themselves, one realizes that the media are well aware of some of the problems, and have already indicated their concern.

Thirdly, look at the media objectively.

Most newspapers, advertisements, and radio and television programmes work by involvement.

A news programme or a political feature can be so involving that it's hard to imagine any other viewpoint. The journalism or production can be so compelling that we miss the fact that we are being guided in our reactions.

There are a number of ways to counteract this.

One excellent approach to the media is to *share the experience with others.* Discuss as much as you can.

It's sometimes a good idea to see a television programme with a group of friends, so you can talk about it afterwards.

A newspaper feature can be a good basis for an extended discussion, especially if somebody in the group knows the subject well or can read it up beforehand.

Another helpful way to approach the media is to *compare and contrast media approaches.*

It's a good idea to vary your newspaper reading.

If you normally read a left-wing paper, read a right-wing one sometimes — and vice versa.

Adopt a similar policy with television. Don't always go to the same pundit for your facts!

It can be very illuminating to scrutinize advertisements for hidden 'messages' — what are they saying about happiness ... about relationships ... about possessions ... about stereotypes (*e.g.* of women, race and social groups)?

If you are a member of a church fellowship or Christian Union, this kind of comparison and contrast can be a very helpful group activity.

Living with the media

Above all, the media are a challenge to our Christian discipleship.

No splits

The media must not be a separate compartment of our lives, because if we are Christians there should *be* no separate compartments.

Jesus didn't just redeem the part of us that goes to church. He redeemed the whole of us. There is no part of our lives that is exempt from his claims, and there is no time or place in which we can temporarily relinquish our Christian faith.

Jesus is the Lord of the whole world. He created it (*Hebrews 1:2*). When we live as Christians, we live in him (*Colossians 2:6*).

So he is Lord of the whole of our lives both because the world is his and because we are his, and the media must be brought within the ambit of his lordship.

What does this mean in practice?

> **There is no time or place in which we can temporarily relinquish our Christian faith.**

It means that the same principles and guidelines apply to living with the media as apply to our choice of friends, our decisions about what we do with our lives, our use of money and possessions, and our use of time.

In Colossians 3, Paul moves completely naturally from theological exploration of the person of Christ, to practical instructions on bringing up children and being a good boss. There's no split.

Having the mind of Christ

If we do bring the media into the ambit of our daily Christian discipleship, what will it involve?

If we are going to be true disciples of Jesus Christ we will learn to do three things.

We will look at the media through Christ's eyes

In chapter three we concluded that having the mind of Christ is not an option, but a command. 'Your attitude should be the same as that of Christ Jesus', says Paul (*Philippians 2:5*), and in the New Testament this principle is applied to all levels of life.

This means that a Christian can never sit back and enjoy a television comedy which relies for its 'fun' on racist stereotyping, or while away a few minutes by relaxing with a tabloid newspaper's account of the sexual antics of a film star's lover.

To do so would mean that we were taking pleasure in something which God grieves over.

At the same time it means that a Christian should be thankful for the work of anybody in the media, Christian or not, who reflects God's love for the world and his anger when sin breaks loose.

So the work of John Pilger, reporting the Cambodian atrocities, or that of Norman Stone, directing television films with a Christian perspective, are work that we should, literally, thank God for.

So too are television's *The Cosby Show,* with its celebration of family life, and Mary Kenny's journalism, which is not ashamed to take a

> A Christian can never sit back and enjoy a television comedy which relies for its 'fun' on racial stereotyping.

moral stand on some of the ambiguous issues of the day.

We won't just be passively involved

The media are not one-way communication channels. If you think the media are important, you have the opportunity to respond to them. You have the opportunity to praise and blame as you think appropriate.

The media take note of public opinion about their product. An advertising campaign that doesn't boost sales is soon dropped. A programme on radio or television which attracts a postbag full of complaints and dissatisfaction will be closely re-evaluated. Letters to newspapers are read by *somebody* in the newspaper offices.

But this can work both ways. If people do not respond positively to the good and compassionate in the media, the media planners may well assume that nobody cares.

There are many ways of making your opinions known. Radio has phone-ins. In at least one, a representative of the broadcasting authority is available for direct questions and comments from the public.

You can talk back to television in a wide range of ways, from *Right to Reply* and *Points of View* to audience-participation programmes such as BBC's *Kilroy* and ITV's *The Time . . . The Place . . .*

Letters to the newspapers and writing direct to companies about their advertisements can also be effective, though you won't receive an acknowledgment every time.

We will consider becoming directly involved

Not very long ago, few Christians worked in the media. Unless you were doing something distinctly Christian, such as religious broadcasting or writing a church column in a newspaper, it was considered by many Christians as something which Christians should not do.

Today it's a very different picture. Christians

> **If people do not respond positively to the good and compassionate, the media planners may well assume that nobody cares.**

are active in radio and television, in journalism, in advertising and in all the media. They are working as writers, producers, editors, artists, graphic designers, and many more.

Very few of them see themselves primarily as missionaries. They regard themselves as professionals. Most are people who are using the gifts which God has given them, in situations which are competitive and challenging.

It's a particularly appropriate workplace for Christians; the media are essentially about communication, and about truth. Both are matters in which Christianity is deeply involved.

So if you are a Christian and are thinking about what to do with your life, the media are certainly a field you should consider.

Books on the media

Neil Postman, *Amusing Ourselves to Death* (Methuen, 1985). An inexpensive and exuberant critique of American television. A sobering read for UK readers, too.

John Ellis, *Visible Fictions: Cinema, Television, Video* (Routledge & Kegan Paul, 1982). A thorough study of the relationship between the three. Ellis talks about how we can evaluate the media, and what our criteria of excellence should be.

Len Masterman, *Teaching the Media* (Comedia, 1985). This book is designed for media studies teachers, and is quite an academic treatment. However, it's full of useful information and revealing insights, and is worth the effort. Masterman is one of the most important academics in the field.

True freedom

We have seen that the media are immensely powerful. Many people feel threatened by them, and few feel entirely comfortable with them.

An old proverb warns that 'the price of freedom is eternal vigilance'. As Christians, we have tremendous freedom. We are in a world which was created by God, designed for our needs. Even though the world has been abused and exploited, it remains God's world, and Jesus is Lord of it.

But freedom follows only from really knowing who God is, and from following Jesus.

This is the reference point which gives us a place to stand, from which we can observe the shifting and volatile patterns of daily life.

If God is truth, we have a standard by which to measure everything.

If God is truth, we have a standard by which to measure *everything*. If Jesus is Lord, and human beings can (as the gospel claims) have a living relationship with him, then it is possible to talk about the world — and its media — to the person who made it.

'If you hold to my teaching,' Jesus promised, 'you are really my disciples. Then you will know the truth, and the truth will set you free' (*John 8:31-32*).

And that includes being set free to explore and enjoy the media.

FRAMEWORKS FOR LIVING
'Direct access to live issues'

David Porter
USER'S GUIDE TO THE MEDIA
How to enjoy and evaluate soaps, adverts, news, the message.
– Don't scrub soap
– What a friend we have in Volkswagon
– I photograph best from the left
– More is said than what is spoken

Joyce Huggett
LIFE IN A SEX-MAD SOCIETY
Handling intimacy, sex and friendship.
– The petting problem
– Cooling the sex urge
– Is sexual sin unforgivable?
– The pain of splitting up

J. John
DEAD SURE? about yourself, life, faith.
A credible explanation of Christianity for today.
– Modern problems
– Anxiety, stress, loneliness
– The Jesus story in modern English
– No resurrection
– No Christianity
– Why believe?

Alan MacDonald with Tony Campolo,
Val Howard and others
THE TIME OF YOUR LIFE
– Getting more from pop and film
– Enjoying sport and friends
– Social times and social action
– The place of drink and parties

Frameworks for living series

Colourful and readable.
Straight to the heart
of today's big issues.

Also released:
Life in a sex-mad society
by Joyce Huggett

FRAMEWORKS
for living

hen you're a single person what
can you do about your desire
for intimacy, embracing . . .'
'We're very much in love. We're
sorely tempted to go too far too soon
physically. . .'
The petting problem — cooling the sex
urge — Is sexual sin unforgivable? —
The pain of splitting up — and much
more.
Direct and wise advice on handling sex
and friendship from the internationally
respected counsellor Joyce Huggett.